*A story of persistence and
inspiration*

By
Elsie Normington

2nd Edition 2013

Published by:
For the Right Reasons 38-40 Grant Street,
Inverness IV3 8BN

Contents

Acknowledgments
Prologue

Dedication

This book is dedicated to my son
Andrew Normington
who is a gift to me, my family and society

Elsie Normington

Acknowledgements

This book has been written over a decade, where I have kept notes of events, so that I would not forget key occasions. I want to thank those who have given me encouragement to eventually bring this book to publication.

Thanks first must go to my daughter Julie Mortimer who spent many hours going through the text and commenting on the memories and emotional journey which I travelled during the difficult years. Thanks also to my sister Elizabeth Norris who proof read the text and gave valuable corrections and encouragement.

Also to my close friend and colleague Liz Syred who provided some very interesting feedback in enabling me to 'pad out' information which I just assumed that everyone would already know, but realised that the subject matter could be new to some readers.

Finally to my friend and mentor of many years, Donald Macleod who has consistently inspired me in my community work and given me insightful direction and professional help with this text.

Without them, the book would not have been completed, so I gratefully acknowledge their time and contributions.

Prologue

I had a happy childhood, was brought up well, loved and cared for in a safe and happy working class family. My father was a miner and my mother was a housewife, cooking good wholesome food, lots of delicious baking, cleaning the house on a regular rotation every week and caring for me and my older sister and brother, living in a three bed-roomed council house. In her spare time she did lots of beautiful crochet. We lived good lives, respected others and worked hard.

My parents were not musicians, but they had an old organ in the sitting room and each of us were sent to organ lessons. I often think about the financial sacrifice that decision was for my mum to send all three of us for 1:1 lessons in Lochgelly which was a 10 minute bus ride from the village of Ballingry, Fife where we lived. We graduated on to a lovely big black shiny piano and all of us still play piano to this day. Each of us did our stint in the local church, playing for the hymns and I remember starting my public playing when I was 14yrs old at the Sunday School Soiree. It was always a great occasion when all the children who attended Sunday School took part in the soiree (concert) and I performed my first public part when I was 4yrs 10 months old singing a solo to the gathered audience. Singing and music has been part of my life since and although I was never going to be a virtuoso classical performer, I loved to sing and get others singing along, while I played piano.

The family home was always filled with my brother and sister's friends round and there would be lots of singing, while Elizabeth or Charles would play piano. I always had to do a solo on these occasions and when I grew into the teenage years I sang in a duet and subsequently a trio with my sister, singing at various events. So music and singing was a very natural and distinctive part of my life and still is to this day.

My teenage years were quite uneventful and I was delighted to fall in love at 19 years old with George who came from Glasgow and we married after a 2 year courtship. Life seemed good, me the mum, George the dad, two children Julie and Andrew and not to forget Misty the dog. We lived in Glasgow for 8 years then moved to Inverness in the Highlands of Scotland.

Little did I know what lay ahead in our family journey when I came to the point of feeling I could not go on! No longer did I want to live with shame, endless tears, feeling misunderstood, isolation and deep grief - day in, day out. I came to a day where I decided that I would end it all. I thought to myself, everyone else can pick up the pieces. I have done much more than my best – for everyone, except myself. I had gone beyond my ability to cope any more. So many demands upon me, I couldn't bear it. Now George is home for the week-end, he can do his share. I believed in God but where is He today? I felt I was done with life. Yes I felt finished, physically, emotionally and spiritually, there was no spirit left to fight and live, I wanted out.

I took my leather shoulder bag and put Andrew's medications into the bag and walked several miles away into the countryside. I came to a small fast flowing river and decided that I would take all of his pills and when I conked out, I would slip into the river and that would be the end. My light would go out, I had done my bit. I felt I had nothing left to give and felt unloved, unappreciated and uncared for by the world.

Sitting there on the banks of the river for several hours, deliberating the thought *'will I do it, can I do it, do I really want to do it, what's driving me to do it, what about my family?'*

All these thoughts were in a mumbo jumbo in my mind, I was so weary and so ashamed. Such was my deep pain and sadness at the black cloud of disappointment that had entered my life. I thought to myself, there must be a way through, but how?

Could my life ever change for the better?

Of all things you must wear
a smile is most important

1. The Early Years

At the end of the school day, the front door swings open and a tall handsome teenager bounds in and throws an enormous hug upon me, which nearly knocks me for six. He says, "*You're here for me mum*". You see, I was not always there for him, because often other people were there for him too.

Twenty seven years ago, I was very much looking forward to the arrival of another baby. We had a six year old beautiful daughter and longed for another sibling for our little family of three – Mum, Dad and Julie. I was so happy to be pregnant, blooming and bouncing along through this joyous time, in anticipation of our second child being born. I had a miscarriage three years before, so I was especially careful, doing everything 'by the book' to ensure my baby would be as healthy as possible.

The miscarriage had really shocked me as I was healthy and active, good diet and harmonious social relationships, how could I miscarry? It was a devastating experience for me and left me feeling emotionally low for a time. I followed everything I had learned about good healthcare, yet this experience felt like it was my fault. I had such a deep sense of let down and failure that I could not retain that precious little foetus in my womb, what on earth is wrong with me? My mood sunk really low and I had a thousand questions swimming around my head which felt unanswered and thought this was unfair. This experience didn't really fit with my life expectations and belief system that I lived by, so how could this happen to me? One church leader told me I did not have enough faith. The doctor said that miscarriages often occurred because the foetus was not developing properly, so it is expelled. It took me ages to get over that experience and get to that place of hope and belief that I would conceive again, and three years later, we did!

My heart danced in tune with every song I've ever sung, knowing that I was pregnant again. Feelings, emotions and thoughts joined in a chorus with all of creation, sensing a delightful harmony that had never been written. I was a happy mum and wife, living in our own little bungalow in the suburbs of Inverness, the gateway to the Highlands. Although money was a bit tight, we had each other and enjoyed our life. I had a really happy and healthy pregnancy, after all I had waited nearly six years for this moment to arrive again in the anticipation of giving birth to another child.

The great day dawned, as the unborn child made his way into the world. He arrived with a quick, sharp and excruciating labour, making his entrance into the delivery room with continuous screaming which seemed an antithesis to the earlier harmony in my world of songs, joy and happiness. Perhaps he was announcing his entry in a celebrationary, triumphal style, ensuring his arrival would not go unnoticed! The midwife weighed him – a bouncing 10lbs and after initial cuddles, she laid him in his little perspex crib in the nursery at Raigmore Hospital, Inverness. This new baby looked like he was three months old, beside all the other new-borns, he was so large.

After hospital discharge, we were becoming accustomed to this newly re-designed family unit. A little brother for Julie and a new son for us parents. Julie fetched and carried, held and cuddled, cooed and giggled with him during those happy days. Regular visits from the District Nurse were supportive and informative, as each day witnessed additional strength and vitality. I was enjoying being the mother of another baby and also watching Julie's enjoyment with her new brother.

The fascinating process of development began to travel its journey and Andrew seemed to be doing well. Holding his head up, grasping little toys, crawling then walking, all within the expected time scales of the Health Visitor's developmental charts. Progress was in order and re-assuring as we journeyed these early months. Feeding was no problem, however, it became apparent that Andrew was allergic to peanuts after a few attempts at peanut butter sandwiches, as he developed a fiery rash. He was also a right screamer at times and my sister was always concerned about 'the high pitch' of his screaming as she was a paediatric nurse. I used to wonder why he had such a high pitched scream, occasionally it would go on for ages before he fell over to sleep. This time round, we used a dummy as Julie sucked her thumb and since you can't take their thumb away, we decided the dummy was the better option, learning from experience.

Language development seemed to be a bit slower. The assumption being made that an older sibling fetches and carries for the younger child, hence there is not the same pressing need to talk. His verbal language did develop in time and he became quite a chatterbox. The predictable mischief and exploration started, pulling objects out of cupboards, climbing into forbidden territory and eating items, which were not palatable. This of course was all part of child development and as diligent parents, we created clear boundaries for discipline and routine, providing a secure environment for social and intellectual growth.

Strangely, he didn't seem too interested in books. We had lots of them, all kinds of books and topics, bookshelves of them. Julie, his sister, loved story times, but not Andrew. He would be happy kicking the ball, playing on the plastic car or riding his plastic digger with a large scoop which he could use to move the sand which was lying around our garden. The reason for having sand in the garden was that we had just built our house, to accommodate my mum, who had become socially isolated and somewhat disabled.

Mum lived in Fife, where I was brought up and had now been a widow for several years. Her health was failing and she had an extended period in hospital due to a severe chest infection. We felt very concerned for her as she was ageing and all the family had left the area. She was really house bound, rarely went out and her life was very narrow indeed. We thought long and hard about what the best route would be to support her in her elder years and decided that if we could build a house we could give her a little bedroom and sitting room. George's cousin had built a couple of houses and encouraged us to do it, as it was much cheaper than buying a bigger house – just a big project which we had never undertaken before.

So we did build a lovely new five bed roomed bungalow. In these days, land was much cheaper and we were able to buy a plot on a small estate in Resaurie at the back of Smithton, Inverness. I had the job of being 'clerk of works' since I was home and had to organise all the building materials and when the different tradesmen would come and do their part of the building. It was a big project and we lived with my sister while it was being done as she lived nearby and we shared all the household stuff together.

Eventually the big day came when we moved in to the house and felt we had really come to our dream house. It had a large lounge/dining room and a large kitchen / diner. I now had a utility room, which was a real luxury and we had five bedrooms with two bathrooms. This meant that my mum had the two bedrooms at the end of the hall and her own little shower room which worked out really well, giving her some privacy but being part of the household.

The children loved to have Gran on hand, who was always ready to listen to them and playing endless little games of cards, lego and cars. She was always willing to baby-sit which was a bonus, having this extended family lifestyle. Her life was simple and content, doing lots of reading, and fine crochet, making beautiful table mats with colourful pansies and took immense patience doing such fine work. She was happy living with us as we all got on well together, even although she was becoming increasingly frail.

George worked as a BT telephone engineer and had done so all of his working life. He is the resilient quiet type, very loyal, consistent and hard working. Our value base came out of a strong working class background, where the 'man was the breadwinner' and the woman had the main domestic responsibilities. My own father was a miner in 'The Mary Colliery' in Lochore and Mum stayed at home to run the house with the three children. Times had changed and although I had given up my career in Civil Service when I left to have my first baby, I had done several part time jobs to fit in with family life, such as party plan selling Tupperware products, worked from home as a Childminder, sold carpets from our garage and even did some Bed & Breakfast during the tourist season. I felt it was really important that I contributed to the family income and it just provided some more funds for little luxuries in life we could not afford.

When Andrew was 2 years old he developed serious asthma and had 7 admissions to hospital during the next 18 months. He would be put on a drip with the medication called Aminophylline to get his breathing under control. One evening we took him along to a special church event where there was a Healing Preacher talking to the crowd. At the end of his talk, he invited people to come for prayer to be healed and we took Andrew and stood patiently in the line. He was sleeping on George's shoulder and as these meetings go for a long time, when it came to our turn, the preacher put his hand on his head and said '*No more asthma. Next*' We thought to ourselves, '*is that it?*' but interestingly enough, the asthma rapidly diminished and by the time he reached 5 years old, he only used the inhaler occasionally.

Andrew reached his significant milestone of three years and started the local playgroup in Smithton Hall. We had sent Julie to a private nursery, but felt that the local playgroup would be appropriate for Andrew where he could learn and develop pre-school skills, as playgroups were now working to national quality standards. Not only that, money was now tighter having four to care for and feed, so this was a much cheaper option.

Time passed and Andrew enjoyed playgroup, having lots of little friends, he enjoyed all the activities and learned to ride a bike. However, he was not interested in books, nor did he want to use a pencil or draw and oftentimes seemed a bit dreamy and unresponsive. At one point, I was convinced he was having some hearing problems as it seemed like he was not hearing me. After a chat with the Health Visitor and subsequently an additional hearing test, I was assured that all was well. However, in my mind, I was not convinced, I didn't like this dreaminess and felt that things were not quite as they should be. He didn't respond to my instructions and especially if I gave more than one instruction, he seemed to have difficulty in following it. Was this a hearing problem, or was it something else I wondered. Little did I know what lay ahead for him and for our family.

Allow failure to be
stepping stones to success

2. The Wind of Change

Happy home and happy days in the Normington family. Life peddled its way along the daily paths of school, playgroup, work and leisure as we lived our contented lives as a family. Off to Playgroup each morning and in the afternoons, Andrew would play with the other pre-schoolers whose parents had also built houses on the small estate of six new builds. It was a paradise of sand, wood, stones and bricks for young children. Many fulfilling hours were spent making all kinds of creations with these materials – always dirty, but happy. There were a few children in our little estate at that time and they all played together.

Saturday was family day and oftentimes we would go for a ramble into the nearby countryside, walking in the shallow burns with our wellingtons, creating our own fun, discovering what would float, examining the wild flowers and listening to the birds. Then came picnic time which was of great interest in choosing the appropriate location, to sit on the luscious grass and enjoy the sensory experience of touching the beautiful lichens, which carpeted these unspoilt woodlands. My nephew Jamie often joined us on these occasions. He was three years younger than Julie and three years older than Andrew, which made a complete, happy group. This gave my sister Elizabeth some time off, being a lone parent and very hard worker. We had many happy occasions enjoying these pastimes which didn't cost us lots of money, which we were short of anyway and it was only a short drive in the car to reach the countryside, which was one of the joys of living in Inverness.

It was around Easter time when Andrew was four and a half years old, he began to have little jerks with his arms. The first time I saw these jerks, I thought he was afraid of something and naturally cuddled and reassured him, but it did seem very strange and unusual to me. It happened numerous times and in fact sometimes he would have several of these jerks in a row. I was mystified by this, so I decided to make an appointment with my GP and tell him all about it. After some careful questioning by the GP, he said that would refer Andrew to a Paediatrician for further tests and consultation.

In the interim, I started keeping a note of these jerky episodes and was astounded at how many he was having on a daily and weekly basis. Sadly, we had to wait nine months for that precious appointment at the Child Clinic in Raigmore Hospital, Inverness. I hope the waiting times are less now a days as that was a *very long wait* for that important appointment. During this time, these jerks were more pronounced, many more of them and occurring more frequently. I was becoming increasingly concerned and really didn't have a clue about what it could mean. My Mum and sister thought I was exaggerating, since I have a slight tendency to do so, as they had not seen these jerks, but when they did see it for themselves, they realised something indeed was seriously wrong with Andrew.

In the August of that year Andrew started school. He settled in well and looked so smart in his little uniform, he being Primary one and his big sister Julie was Primary seven. It was only five minutes walk along the road and after several months, I thought he was able to go on his own, like the other local children. At Christmas time, he sang a solo in the Christmas service in front of over one hundred people, so I was reasonably happy that he was growing and developing, yet still had these nagging thoughts about all of these jerks he kept having every day. Whatever could they be, what could this mean, when would I get that precious appointment and what would they tell me, so my thoughts went round and round in my mind.

Strangely, Andrew did not seem to understand some of the basic concepts in his education. The little tin of words which were sent home, held no interest for him and I, trying to be a diligent mother, was insistent that he would remember his words 'in his tin'. It seemed like, his mind was becoming a bit hazy somehow, in fact he was forgetting some basic words like sock and shoe or fork and knife. I remember on one occasion when I was getting quite exasperated that he was forgetting simple words and I took a sock which was drying on the radiator and asked him *"what is this"*. He obviously could not remember and ran up the five stairs to Gran's little sitting room asking her *"Gran what is this?"* He then ran back and said to me *"Mum it is a sock"*. I recall running into the bathroom and bursting into tears thinking, *"how does Andrew not remember the word sock anymore"*. What is wrong with him?"

I was becoming increasingly concerned about these 'jerks' and now concerned about his education. After raising concerns with the class teacher, she assured me that *'all children learn at a different pace and not to be too concerned'*. Once again, I was not convinced by her response and decided to start walking with him every day to and from school, which seemed like a regressive step, as my nephew had seen him wandering around, appearing confused after one school day had finished. This sounded a bit worrying to me as he had been able to walk home before but he appeared quite confused at times, so I decided to 'play safe' and take him back and forward the short walk to school myself. This did not fit well with my beliefs and attitude to life, where children are taught to become independent and responsible for themselves.

At last, the important piece of mail arrived through my letter box – an appointment with the Paediatric Clinic at Raigmore Hospital. It was a very busy clinic and fortunately there was a little room with toys, as we had to wait forty minutes before we were taken for our appointment, which for me seemed like an eternity. The Paediatrician was a real gentleman, poised, thoughtful, good listening skills and sat at his desk with excellent posture, his white hair receding back into his high brow.

I had taken a little list of questions and prompts as I was nervous about the appointment, rarely being in a hospital environment and not really knowing what to expect. However the Paediatrician gave us the time we needed and the conclusion was that Andrew should have an EEG done. An appointment would be made again at the clinic when the results of this test were processed. He explained to me that this test was called an Electroencephalogram, which is a machine examining how the brain behaves and can differentiate between normal and abnormal brainwave patterns.

Several more weeks passed until we received an appointment to have the EEG done which felt like another very long wait. When we were taken for the appointment, I was quite amazed at Andrew's compliance as the technician attached the 20 electrodes on to Andrew's head and then he had to lie down on the bed for 30 minutes while the machine did its work. The electrodes were attached to a large machine, which had a huge roll of paper and the wave patterns were printing out spikes and waves all along the sheet. Of course this meant nothing to me as I sat patiently waiting, longing, for some kind of explanation, hoping it would all disappear. However, I have to say that I didn't like the way the machine was behaving! It would have several consistent patterns then suddenly it seemed to go very squiggly for a couple of minutes, then go back to the consistent patterns again and so this went on throughout the whole test. The test was complete and the technician removed all the electrodes from his head and told me that we would get the results from the Paediatrician in due course. Oh well, this would be yet another long wait.

Several more weeks passed again until I saw the Consultant Paediatrician gentleman who informed me that the EEG had shown up *considerable abnormality* in the brain wave patterns, which explained to me all these big squiggly patterns at the EEG test, and as a result, Andrew was diagnosed with epilepsy. He said that medication would be required and we should return in three months to the clinic. I drove home, thinking deeply and reflecting on his words. Epilepsy. What does this mean?

I only knew of one other person who had epilepsy and he was married, had a professional job and seemed to be getting along well in life. Perhaps it would be the same for Andrew, once the medication starting working, he would be fine. I had no knowledge of epilepsy. I didn't know at that time that often people have EEG tests done and no abnormality shows up, as lots of people that have the epilepsy diagnosis may only have seizures now and then. This was new terminology to me, a new world I had entered and didn't know the direction, the language or the pathway it would take.

Andrew was not fine. In fact, things began to go from bad to worse. These 'jerks' as I had called them, were called Myoclonic Seizures and they became more and more frequent, in fact they now came in clusters, which meant that he would have several at a time and sometimes several series of them within a day. New 'jerks' started which seemed more pronounced where his arms would stiffen and then he would appear to be in some form of automatic behaviour which I later discovered was called Automatism, as if he was detached from the real world. Sometimes he required to sleep afterwards. These were called Complex Partial Seizures.

Attending the Paediatric clinic was becoming a regular occurrence although I still felt enormously inadequate, nervous, confused and worried, not really knowing what questions to ask and very concerned as to how this condition seemed to be worsening and running its course. On one occasion, I took my sister with me as I felt that I needed some moral support to go along to this hospital clinic. Other occasions I would have my little notebook with prompts to ask questions as I urgently needed answers to make sense of this nightmare journey I was travelling on, which I had not chosen nor wanted.

On one occasion, Andrew had one of his Myoclonic clusters while in the Consultant's clinic and the Paediatrician and his fascinated student watched with intense interest. I thought, *Was this so unusual? Why couldn't it be stopped? Isn't there medication, which will make him OK? Please can he progress his education?* I had a thousand questions – most of which didn't seem to have answers at this stage. A cocktail of anti-convulsant medication had now been tried which seemed of little or no help for his condition. In fact some of the medications prescribed, particularly Clonazepam caused horrific mood swings and I felt like I had lost the little happy boy that had grown through his pre-school years. His behaviour often appeared like a light switch going off and on, such were the mood swings that he experienced. This was no longer the happy little Andrew I once had in my precious family. What on earth was happening to him?

During that time we went to Oxford to visit our dear friends Derek and Anne Daley. Derek was the accountant for a large boys school and they lived on site. They had come to Inverness on holiday as I did *Bed & Breakfast* for a couple of months in the summer to try and make some extra income for the family and they had become family friends. While we had our holiday at Oxford, Derek and Anne were very kind to us and we had a lovely time. They took us in the train to London and showed us the sights. They also took us to Henley and various beautiful parts around the area. However, my recollection of that lovely holiday was the fact that Andrew's behaviour was particularly unpredictable and his mood was deeply affected by the Clonazepam medication as it was like turning the switch off and on, such rapid changes and so unexpected, my dear son, what were we doing to you with all these medications which were being tried to control these seizures? It certainly was not working and in fact it seemed to be getting worse and worse by the day and the medication was not taking effect. My heart ached so badly, I was so sad and confused with the constant nagging question "What's wrong with him?" Yes, they told me epilepsy, but is this what epilepsy is really like in real everyday life, where there is regression, mood swings and endless seizures day and night?

The local primary school were now making comments about Andrew requiring some extra help. My immediate thought was *'please don't keep him back a year'*. I discovered that was not current proceedure, it was all about identifying his needs and how he could be appropriately supported in his education. One vivid memory was the occasion when I was invited into the school to a meeting with the Head of the Infant Department. She was a kind teacher, who cared and understood, yet at the same time, was immensely professional. She told me that Andrew had learning difficulties and required extra support. The plan was to have him join a little special unit within the school, where there were other children who had learning difficulties too and he would be integrated with his peers for subjects like music, art and PE.

Once again, I returned home thinking deeply and reflecting on her words. Learning difficulties. What did learning difficulties mean? Was he just slow? But how could he be slow? My husband and I are reasonably intelligent. How could this possibly be right? Yet, this lovely teacher has worked with children all her life, she must be informed in making this kind of judgement about his ability. I didn't understand how he could have learning difficulties, whatever the term really meant, after all I was a good parent, committed to good parenting in every way, diligent and always sought to do the right things in life. My heart was so heavy at this news, in fact it was pounding with fears and concerns at hearing these words. I was in disbelief, this can't be right! I was scared, frightened as I didn't know what it could mean. I couldn't comprehend the term and the implications of it – words like 'mentally handicapped' and 'mentally retarded' sprung to mind, that's what people called children who were very mentally disabled. Was Andrew going to be like that? He didn't look like it, yet he lived in his own world rather a lot....often talking away to himself in his bedroom, but not talking much to other people. How's that I wondered?

Things are not right, but learning difficulties? I didn't know anyone else who had a child that had learning difficulties. How was it that Andrew was given this tag. My inner being was swimming with multitudes of unanswered questions and more questions and still more questions and my heart raced with concern as to where this was leading, a special unit, not in the main class. How can he not do the work in the main class? He has already been in the main class. How not now? Why not? Is this what epilepsy does to a person? I didn't know that would happen after the epilepsy diagnosis! This is not fair, it's not right. I've lived a good life and been a good mum, how can this happen and so my inner ranting went on and on, feeling immense isolation and having no-on to turn to and talk about this inner journey of new information that had, so unexpectedly landed on my lap.

All of my friends had kids at school and they were all getting on fine. When we all got together, Andrew was usually left out, why was that? Did he not understand the games? Was he just happy on his own? I don't think so, we all need to connect with our peers. What was different about him? I only hoped, surely, surely, things will turn out all right for Andrew. This will pass, surely it's just a blip, the epilepsy and the learning difficulties will get better - but they didn't.

*Our focus in life
will determine our level of happiness*

3. Family Demands

Life does not stand still, it moves on. Children grow, adults change and older people often become frail and so it was in our home.

Julie was now a teenager and pushing every boundary, which surrounded her life. She was into rebellion, had developed an attitude and wasn't really following our normal family lifestyle. I found that my role was changing rapidly and was living in quite a different world to the cosy one I had set out with, in these early marital years. My teenage daughter had been a delight to bring up through her childhood years, but now the relationship, perceptions and family values were being challenged through various responses and the dreams I had for her were suddenly in a vortex swirling around into oblivion.

However, I always had a book on the go and read about the importance of loving our teenager but not their behaviour. I took Julie off on 'girlie trips' now and then. One particular trip was a week-end away on the train to Lincoln where there was some beautiful architecture, as Julie seemed to be interested in architecture and graphic design. She had been trying out smoking cigarettes and had terrible headaches, since she wasn't smoking with me on the week-end! Thankfully that was a passing phase. However, I have a lovely picture of Lincoln Cathedral hung in my hallway at home and I had it framed as it always reminds me of the importance of loving my teenager despite her behaviour. Not only that, it is so important to ensure all the family members are loved and nurtured, as there is a distinctive danger that the disabled child gets all the attention from the parents and siblings can be left a bit on the side. I made sure that would not happen with Julie. She does, often refer to these trips we did together and if you are a Mum with a child who has special needs, I encourage you to ensure that you give lots of attention to the other siblings. We are great friends today and love to be together, especially doing 'girly things' like retail therapy, pamper stuff and going to see a West End Musical in London.

During that special trip to Lincoln, I remember visiting a historic building which used to be an old Sanatorium where people were cared for, mostly people who were mentally retarded as they called it in these days. I distinctly remember reading about people who had epilepsy and they were taken to the local sheriff court and certified as 'mad' then relegated to this Sanatorium. They had drawings on information boards of how these people were cared for and some were chained to beds and chairs because of their seizures jerking.........how awful! I thought to myself how thankful I was for my little son Andrew that he had been born in the 20th century and not the previous century or he would have been treated in this way.

My brother Charles, who is single had been on long term missionary work was at a crossroads in his life and came to stay with us for a period of reflection and restoration, which ended up being nine months. He did lots of odd jobs around the house, which kept him occupied and we appreciated his DIY skills, but it was someone else in the house at that time, who needed a bit of support and also another person at the table being fed, cared for and supported.

Mum was becoming increasingly disabled and required more support. She had lots of chest problems and arthritis, which restricted her personal independence. She rarely went out and was happy and contented to be at home. I tried to get her into the McKenzie Centre which is a Day Centre for older people but she was not keen on that idea, plus I would have to transport her there and back which would be yet another demand for my already overworked day. I had to do all the cooking of course, shopping, all the housework, washing and ironing and attend to all of mum's personal messages, as well as wash her lovely long white silvery hair every week and dry it for her.

George had been working all over the Highlands doing relief work, so he was only home at week-ends, although he faithfully phoned me every evening. He had his journey too, of coming to terms with teenage tantrums, disability diagnosis, and caring concerns. However, I really grudged him being away and me being left to everything. Most days when I turned up at school to collect Andrew, the teacher would be waiting at the door to tell me what had happened that day – seizures sometimes followed by incontinence, confusion, automatisms and frequently having to sleep for an hour or two. I felt so scared by all of this information and was so reluctant to collect him each day, wondering what the latest scenario would be from the teacher. I really didn't know how to cope with it all. Every day, there seemed to be more and more and more. More information, more bad news, more demands upon me, both physically and emotionally, everything piling up into a huge mountain of stresses and demands.

I was also working as a private piano teacher by this time – a job I loved. It was fascinating how my little business began. One day, a local mum in the area asked me if I would teach piano to her daughter as she didn't have a car to take her to another teacher who lived two miles away. I initially declined her offer, but she was persistent, so I reluctantly started to teach piano and to my surprise I really enjoyed it. As a result, I went back to piano lessons myself and started at grade four and worked through all the levels to grade eight piano and music theory. By that time, I really felt that I had a good handle on all the practical and theory which would enable me to have credibility in teaching others, even although I had played piano from my childhood years. Therefore this new development of teaching people to play piano in some ways seemed a natural transition for me.

Each pupil would ring the doorbell and walk in for their lesson at half hour intervals and I would put them through their musical paces. It gave me great pleasure to observe all of my pupils' progress and have them all take part in my annual concert called *"Tune In"* where we raised funds for local charities. Music was my passion and I loved to teach and pass on what I knew to others. Many of the pupils passed a number of piano and theory exams and some went on to study a degree in music, which I thought was quite wonderful, to surpass their first piano teacher! I also taught adults as most local teachers at that time only taught children and teenagers, so very quickly I ended up with a waiting list for my piano tuition.

I was also very involved in church, leading the Worship Band and the Puppet Team, also supporting my husband in pastoral issues. Later I became the Creative Ministry Leader and life was very full indeed. We had to attend lots of church related meetings and at times, it felt like there would never be enough hours in life to accomplish all these expectations. If we weren't at church leader's meetings, we were attending church meetings or we were preparing to talk or lead a meeting. So life raced on with all these varied family demands, working part time and lots of involvement in the church and in the midst of this,

Andrew's condition worsened and there were lots of education and health meetings to attend about his condition.

One day I met an old friend who was a speech and language therapist. She enquired after Andrew and I poured out my tale of woe. Her advice to me was that I should write to Psychological Services in the Education Department and ask for a 'Record of Needs' to be opened. This was more new language to me – 'Record of Needs' (RON) what did this mean? She told me that it was important for children who had special needs to have a RON which would state their requirements to have their educational needs being met. I had no understanding about the assessment process for the RON, but thought it sounded like a good idea to pursue her advice. I duly wrote to the Education Psychology Department, explaining Andrew's condition highlighting his apparent regression in educational attainment. Nowadays the terms have all changed and they write a 'Child's Plan' which incorporates the Individual Education Plan.

The Educational Psychologist contacted us quite quickly after my letter had been sent and informed us that she would assess Andrew in school. She then came to visit us at our home with her results. I discovered that the Educational Psychologist was different to a Clinical Psychologist. The Education Psychologist assess and give advice regarding children who have educational problems such as learning difficulties, dyslexia and emotional and behavioural problems and are usually employed by the Local Authority. The Clinical Psychologist is concerned with all aspects of behaviour and the thoughts, feelings and motivation underlying behaviours, they often work for NHS or Private Practices.

So our Educational Psychologist arrived and was professional with a friendly tone, telling us that she had assessed Andrew and had found he had moderate learning difficulties. I had heard about learning difficulties, still trying to understand its meaning – now it was 'moderate'. I asked her what this term meant. She explained that he was at the "*bottom end of mainstream school and top end of special school*". The words were out. They were spoken - SPECIAL SCHOOL? Oh Surely not. No. I can't believe this could possibly be true. I thought he was just a bit slow? Surely he would never be in a special school! I thought special school was for children who were severely disabled. Andrew was not severely disabled, was he? Or was he, or could he be going that way? Oh no, surely not. I really did not want to believe this was happening.

She explained that the connection with his epilepsy made it difficult to give a clear assessment as his difficulties could vary, depending on the seizure activity happening at a given time, but felt that he could be supported well within the mainstream school. His seizure disorder was complex which meant that some days he would be dull and other days he would be brighter and interacting better with the class work, so indeed I could understand that this was a difficult task for her to give a true assessment because of the complexity of the epilepsy.

We said goodbye and the door closed behind her. Disbelief, confusion, shock and sadness seriously hit my emotions like a boxer punching his bag. I was reeling with the words '*special school*' this inferred a whole new, different, unexpected meaning to Andrew's education, his life, and indeed our lives as a family.

What did all of this mean? The epilepsy is worsening, as was his educational abililty. I often listened to him outside his bedroom door, talking incessantly to himself in his bedroom, yet he became slower in speaking to us, or anyone else for that matter. Why was he doing this, behaving strangely and regressing in his verbal interactions with us, I just couldn't understand what was happening and of course there was no internet at that time to be researching all of this stuff. I tried to find books about it, to educate myself. What's wrong with him? I read books about epilepsy but it seemed like most people seemed to have their seizures controlled with the right medication. Why is it not being cured or at least controlled better? Why was he having more and more seizures and regressing in his skills and abilities. So many questions unanswered. My heart fainted within me, I felt so helpless as I tried to grapple with these many issues and no-one to share it with, no-one else who could understand what it was like to have a child with epilepsy and learning difficulties. I felt so immensely and so enormously alone in this big world of over six billion people. So misunderstood, felt on the outside and so alone.

After the assessment with the Educational Psychologist, the process then began to open a 'Record of Needs' which was an official document stating what Andrew's educational needs were and how they would be met. They sent us a draft copy which we had to sign and also give a 'named person' who could come along to meetings which reviewed the 'Record of Needs'. These review meetings were annual and each professional would give their comments at the meeting. I found these meetings very intimidating as I was not used to attending meetings around polished tables with a range of professionals discussing my son's condition and how he was responding to all the interventions that had been put in place. I felt totally daunted hearing all the reports about my lovely little boy Andrew, as if he was a piece of public property for all those professionals to sit round and discuss with suggestions of how his little life could be improved.

I felt like an onlooker, gazing into a window of our family's life, being assessed, commented on and at times felt judged or disbelieved. The privacy of family life was no longer the safe little nest where we were the ideal 2.4 family with the dog, but now we were a family who had a son with learning difficulties and complex epilepsy that needed lots of support. How my heart broke, how let down I felt, how I tried to be strong and confident and yet within the walls of my emotional world, I was stretched beyond capacity, felt imprisoned by huge brick walls with no way out and my tears flowed like rapids on an angry river.

By this time, Andrew had a speech and language therapist to help him with his verbal communication as this had extensively regressed. Andrew had gone from being an amusing little chatterbox of a boy who could sing in front of a hundred or more people, to this very quiet boy who chose to speak only when he was able, if seizure activity was dull and not in its rampant state. He had involvement with the school nurse, the class teacher or learning support teacher, the head teacher, educational psychologist and occupational therapist. The community nurse, who also had input about his bowel problems as the medication was causing havoc in that area too and latterly social work were there also. So there were a range of professionals around the table and I found these meetings really emotionally draining, although everyone was usually very respectful within their professional roles.

Three monthly visits to the Paediatric Clinic were now a regular slot, but it really felt like it was going nowhere. All these medications, but none of them seemed to be working, or at least were not controlling the seizures. New seizures were now beginning to emerge, where he was regularly falling down and sometimes incontinent when he collapsed on the floor. This was particularly worrying as I really hadn't a clue as to what to do. I was terrified on these occasions thinking he was going to die with one of those awful seizures when he fell down and his whole body shook and convulsed with such force.

I felt so powerless, desperately wanting the seizure to stop and the two minute time of convulsing with his arms, legs and body writhing and jerking furiously, while saliva oozed from his mouth with a strange noise in his throat, would feel like an eternity of time to me. He would often have a seizure in the morning before going to school, or while having his breakfast and I was frightened he would choke if the seizure came in the middle of eating the breakfast! No-one offered me any coaching on how to manage the epilepsy, I just had to struggle along on my own, doing what I thought best. Once again, I felt so alone, nobody to talk with and share how they managed this condition. Interestingly enough, the professionals and carers seemed to get all the training courses, but here was me working with Andrew every day and night, but I didn't seem to get any training opportunity. Not only that, he also had a severe nut allergy. I remember one occasion where friends had invited us over to their home for dinner. The hostess had a pudding which had nuts on the top and she scraped them off the top of his pudding. Well that wasn't enough, because within ten minutes Andrew's body was covered in a very fiery rash, his lips swelled and his breathing became very laboured. We had to make a quick exit and get him home and give him medication. This was just another issue to look out for on top of everything else.

I began to sense that we needed another opinion about the epilepsy, but was enormously nervous at that thought of speaking to the distinguished Paediatrician gentleman and tell him that I wanted another doctor's view. I needed lots of encouragement to take this step. Although I was quite a confident person, the whole hospital environment and people with lots of high class professional qualifications daunted me and I felt just ' a little Mum' so asking for a referral was a huge step for me to take. Eventually I did take the step and asked for a referral to Yorkhill Children's Hospital in Glasgow to gain a second opinion.

It was another long wait for the appointment in Glasgow. Eventually the appointment came through to see a Paediatric Neurologist at the Yorkhill Clinic where they did a wide variety of tests and finally diagnosed Andrew with Lennox- Gastaut Epilepsy Syndrome. Apparently the prognosis was very poor and it would be unlikely if the epilepsy would ever be controlled. The Paediatric Neurologist suggested trying a ketogenic diet and also explore some other anti-convulsant medication. In the car park of Yorkhill Hospital, I said to George "I am not accepting this diagnosis, I must go to the top of the profession to get a full diagnosis". I just could not accept what I had heard in the clinic.

Once again, shock impacted my emotions to such a degree of force like a hurricane wind blasting through tall trees and strong buildings, leaving behind a trail of carnage and destruction. I felt the deep devastation of pain, disbelief and confusion. Not only was it epilepsy, it was learning difficulties, it was regression in learning, it was unusual behaviours, it was daily medication and now it was some kind of epilepsy syndrome which may never be controlled? I felt like shouting and screaming at the top of my lungs - I can't believe it, how can it be true!

The ketogenic diet they recommended is based on the principle of high fat and low carbohydrate and done under the supervision of a dietician. The clinic gave us a 'special dispensation' due to my other caring responsibilities with my mum and was allowed to pursue this specialised diet at home rather than in hospital. Andrew had to drink a very unsavoury liquid called 'liquigen' and I had to check his urine regularly to establish that he was in ketosis, when the body breaks down fat cells and produces acidic substances, called ketones. This can create a metabolic state, which can prevent seizures. The diet did not work for Andrew as he continued to have the regular seizures. So we had to give up on that option as a cure.

I also visited a Doctor in Kingussie who was an ex-Great Ormond Street Doctor and passionate about vitamin therapy. She suggested that we give Andrew Pyridoxine (Vitamin B6) as seizures can be an indicator of this vitamin deficiency. This regime was also followed fastidiously, but unfortunately effected no improvement for him.

My determination was high, that I would find a cure somewhere for Andrew. I so longed and prayed for him every day that somehow we would find a cure. For a season, the church elders came and prayed for him faithfully every week. I had a handkerchief which was anointed with oil which I kept under his pillow. Then one lady went off to Birmingham to a large convention and she took one of Andrew's T shirts with her and someone told her 'there is a miracle was on the T shirt' so I was pretty excited expecting the miracle to happen soon – again having it under his pillow, but no miracle came. I took him to lots and lots of church meetings but it didn't seem to bring Andrew the healing I expected. Not only was I trying to come to terms with Andrew's complex condition, but my faith and beliefs were being challenged and tested on all fronts, since all the prayers were not yielding the results I expected.

Smithton Primary School staff were wonderful in coping with all of these seizures and they had a quiet corner where Andrew could curl up and sleep off the seizure. I was immensely grateful for this support, as I had heard of other mums with children in other schools who were constantly called by the school to come and take their child home. The staff endeavoured to maximise his 'brighter moments' but as one teacher said at a review, she felt that he was *'marking time'* - in other words not progressing in his education. There were times when he would have a seizure and then run out of the classroom and along the corridor in an automated state. There were six children in the special unit, all different ages and the teacher was absolutely exceptional at accommodating for their individual needs. She truly was an 'extra mile' teacher and I was so thankful for her.

I had heard about Drummond Special School taking the children down to Drumnadrochit Stables for riding lessons and thought that this may be therapeutic for Andrew and also teach him some practical skills. After I made initial enquiries with both schools it was agreed that Andrew could join a peer group with Drummond and attend a riding session. However, I had to drive him over to Drummond School and collect him on his return. The first shock was the yellow mini bus. I don't know what I had imagined, but somehow it reinforced disability to me. Secondly, as I was watching all of the children boarding the bus, with all kinds of disabilities, I was thinking *"does Andrew belong there? They all seemed really disabled"*. Did he fit into this category? He was *so happy* going off on that mini bus with all the other children, waving enthusiastically to me as they drove off......but my eyes were overflowing with tears as I drove the car back home, while he was on his trip. Why was I so upset, yet he was so happy? Why was I so sad on such a happy day for him? He was happy in his world, but I was very unhappy in my world. Things were not turning out as I had planned when I got happily married and we planned to have our little family.

The day came when it was time for the special unit in Smithton School to be closed, some children having moved on, others integrated back into classroom life - which would be the case for Andrew. We were now very seriously looking at his educational future and where he belonged. Another annual review was convened and Andrew was now diagnosed with 'severe learning difficulties' so things were truly regressing and Andrew was not developing as expected. The gap in his development was becoming increasingly obvious and the developmental delay was now considerable. This was yet another blow, as he had gone from 'moderate learning difficulties' to 'severe learning difficulties'. It was becoming more apparent to us that perhaps mainstream school was not going to best meet his needs in the future.

*There are many shadows, but remember,
where there is a shadow there must be a light*

4. Coping with loss

Andrew was now eight years old and this journey of epilepsy had been in motion for four years with all its accompanying problems. I felt no-one in my peer group understood me and my situation. People always asked me 'how Andrew was doing' and no-one asked 'how I was doing'. I felt locked out of the world which continued on its merry way, business as usual, yet I felt ostracised from mainstream normality. I was existing within the framework of day to day routines and necessities but my emotional world was living somewhere else, preoccupied with the big questions, feeling lost and very alone.

I had fallen into a dark cave of despair, with no lights, no hope, just darkness. I felt alone yet I had extended family and many friends. The *isolation* was the worst issue to deal with, not having anyone who knew what it was like to cope with the fear of death, choking, communication impairment, learning difficulties, toileting problems and ongoing sleeplessness. Also having to deal with endless appointments with a range of professionals was such an invasion into my family life, I found it untenable and didn't want all this stuff to deal with in my life any more.

The darkness I felt was black, thick blackness with no light and no hope. There was such a sense of despair and disappointment as this was not what I had signed up for in my life, certainly not what I expected and could not understand how this could happen to me. I felt a personal sense of defeat that I could not seem to find a cure and tried so hard to learn about the condition and try out different suggestions but it seemed like nothing worked, the condition got worse and as one doctor said to me "*the epilepsy is running its course*" and so the list would go on

– endless tears which flowed like a fountain that never was turned off at the mains. I would waken up most nights in the middle of the night and go through to the lounge and cry and cry and cry. I wanted this nightmare to stop. I wanted to rub it out and start again, it can't be true, perhaps I am in a terrible dream and I will wake again and everything will be ok. But no, that was not the case and all the negative emotions were tied around me like the massive thickly bound ropes which holds the ship to the harbour pier, huge ropes of depression, failure, anxiety, stress, worry, concern, confusion, disbelief, disillusionment, grief, loneliness, isolation all bound round me so tightly with endless questions, questions and more questions, all remaining unanswered.

I felt guilty and ashamed that my son would drop down with a seizure anywhere, at any time and sometimes appear to behave in a socially dysfunctional manner. Wherever I went, I found myself always explaining to people what was happening when I got strange looks of questioning or misunderstanding. Somehow, I could not come to terms with this sense of guilt? What had I done wrong that this could happen? I had a spiritual dilemma trying to understand and make sense of what was happening in my life and family. Andrew's condition continued down the slippery slope of regression with uncontrolled seizure activity. The seizures would occur at any time and regularly through the night. I kept hoping that someone, somewhere would have the cure or even to achieve the medication control to keep the seizures at bay. I had difficulty sleeping, my thoughts were in constant turmoil and I was worried about Andrew having seizures and wandering about the house in the middle of the night. In fact one night when he got up at 4am he let the dog out into the garden, who started barking at the top of her lungs!

I knew I was very depressed. Millions of tears poured down my ashen face more times than I care to remember. Often, during the night when I could not sleep, I would come through to the lounge and sit on the couch gazing aimlessly across the field towards the orange lights of the Kessock Bridge and shedding their light on the pretty village of North Kessock, this image which somehow warmed my sad heart. Little did I know that one day I would live in North Kessock. I felt desperately misunderstood, because Andrew was such a handsome lad with his dark hair and dark brown eyes and didn't *look* disabled. People would regularly comment that *'he looked fine'*. It made me feel I was being neurotic or sensationalising his condition. *Yet I knew that things were not fine.*

One day, I was reading in a 'thought for the day' booklet which said *"He will yet fill your mouth with laughter and your lips with shouts of joy"*. Could this be really possible that I could laugh again? It seemed impossible as I was so, so low. In fact, one Saturday I had gone for a long walk into the countryside on my own, after an argument with my husband and taken most of Andrew's medication with me, as I planned to swallow the lot, then slip into the river and end it all. I had come to the point that I could not live life any longer. The demands were too great. Too many people to look after, care for, and too many problems, issues and meetings to go, I just could not manage to do life any more. My physical and emotional reserves had run dry and I could not find anywhere to fill my life tank. I didn't seem to get any time to myself in any shape or form, it was all work at home, work to earn some money to help with family finances, work with endless amounts of church meetings and commitments and also attending all these meetings with Health and Educational

Professionals was very hard work. So there was nothing there for me to recoup my personal resources. This is such an important point, that I want to linger here for a moment. If I only knew then what I know now! The Carers must care for themselves. This was a hugely important lesson that I learned during my journey towards wholeness. I had to learn to prioritise time for me and enjoy fun and creative activities in order to retain a strong sense of well being strength and resilience to continue running the family home.

I thought for a very long time that day as I sat beside the river on my own with all the medication in the bag. I could take all of these pills and thought to myself, as I become drowsy, I would slip into the river and be no more. Someone else would have to pick up the pieces as I had been working the pieces for too long. I felt no-one cared and now, did I really care about myself? I was even losing the drive and self respect for myself. Normally I was such an enthusiastic and driven character, leading and inspiring others, but that day was my blackest day when I almost gave up the precious gift of life.

My cave was very dark indeed, I wanted to give up on life and end it, as I had nothing left to give – I felt that life had drained me and nothing was left, even the tiny spark of hope had been snuffed out when I ran out of new cures to try for Andrew. The negative emotions totally engulfed me in my isolated grieving hut where I barely existed in my emotions, yet carried on with a bright smile out in the world. However, after several hours of deliberation by the river, I decided that my family really needed me, I could not do this to them, so I very reluctantly and slowly walked the long route back home, for them, not for me.

The grief weighed me down to such an extent that I knew I had to visit my GP. I was becoming lethargic and disinterested in life, which was distinctly the opposite to my normal energetic disposition. I did not want to get out of bed and face another day, although I had to get the family cared for and organised, I had to force myself to do these daily tasks. Writing lists was a regular feature of my life, to remind me of everything that had to be done or bought, so I had written down a list of twenty one symptoms that I was experiencing when I went to see my GP. He diagnosed me with clinical depression and offered some medication or Clinical Psychology.

My mother was always into Homeopathic remedies and alternative treatments, so as I grew into adulthood, I always looked for alternative approaches to health and well being. I was therefore somewhat reluctant to take any medication and preferred to take vitamins and power foods.

On this occasion, I opted for Clinical Psychology to see if talking to a professional may bring me some emotional relief. After waiting some time for an appointment with the Clinical Psychologist, I attended for my first appointment. Very quickly, I realised that this man knew and understood the multiple issues I was coping with and began to paint them in a conversational frame. I came out feeling just a little improved and a glimmer of hope began to infiltrate my weary, flagging mind. Three psychology sessions passed and I felt a bit more positive. I began to understand the impact of learning disability on the life of our family and future implications. I was starting to understand that the son I had given birth to was not the learning disabled son I now had. The psychologist was an excellent listener and was highly skilled in asking poignant questions which made me consider tangents I hadn't previously thought about. One question he asked me was *"what is the worst possible thing which could happen"?* This helped me to think through the aspects of concern and worry, whether real or imagined and I began to develop emotional strategies as coping mechanisms in a variety of social situations.

I knew no-one else that had a child with epilepsy or learning difficulties. I felt unique in my journey and didn't know where to turn for moral support. My friends were all really nice but none of them knew what *this* was like – all of their children growing up, learning, developing and talking about their latest achievements. I had a son that was regressing and requiring more and more personal care rather than watching the developmental journey to independence. What could I say about him and yet I wanted to belong and also wanted him to belong as well. Finding this balance was a major challenge in social relationships.

I began to improve in my mood, understanding what had happened in my expectations of life – the fact that the goalposts had moved, it was a new game with new rules, new language and new guidelines. I had to learn all of this in order to play in the game of life. I wanted to enjoy life, but now it seemed like a different country with a new culture and I had to get used to it. This is called acceptance. Until now, I had been in shock, denial, depression and anger, but now it was now time to enter the last stage, which was acceptance. I did not know at the time that this is a classic model which represents the various stages of grief and loss. In fact, I had gone through the first four stages and visiting the Psychologist enabled me to see the way forward into acceptance of the new life with all its challenges, and to go forward in new and fresh strength. Grief and loss is usually associated with bereavement, a loved one who has passed away and the grieving person goes through these stages. However, I began to learn, that I too had gone through the grief and loss of losing the child that I had waited for, for six years, and then that child is not who I thought he was, but in fact was my lovely Andrew who required a different kind of care to support him through his life. I began to see him in a different light and although I always loved both my children, I began to love him *for who he was,* not *who I wanted him to be.*

I also had to come to terms with forgiveness and realise what a powerful tool it is, but I had not applied it to my situation. I was so angry at the lack of information and support given to me through these few years as the epilepsy ran its course. No-one told me how to deal with the seizures; no-one told me what 'learning difficulties' meant and what the range was; no-one told me about what benefits we could claim, as we went for years not claiming additional benefits which we were entitled to; no-one told me about accessing respite for Andrew and for Mum. It felt like any information I found was purely stumbling on little fragments along the way. Thankfully, Information Services are much improved from these days but I was angry inside. Angry at all the professionals for not giving me the information I should have had and also angry at the church, listening to endless sermons on divine healing and constantly being let down. I was also angry at myself for becoming so depressed and not being 'the superwoman' I thought I was, yes I was ANGRY ANGRY and I needed to get rid of this negative energy out of my system!

Little did I realise the power of simply starting to say on a regular basis *"I forgive all those who I believe to have wronged me and I forgive myself".* So often people can live in an emotional prison which they themselves have created, unaware that they have the key to open the prison and walk out. It's a powerful tool and I try to use it most days, if I get angry about any little thing, as I do not want to live in anger again. I want to live in emotional freedom for the remainder of my days. I also tell others when I am delivering life coaching to clients, that forgiveness can bring about powerful emotional freedom and enables us to release the past and let go.

The Health, Education and Social Work professionals were all going about their daily tasks doing their best – it was ME who needed to change and that resolve to change is crucial in the journey to emotional wholeness. There is no point in continually ruminating over the past, living in regret, going over the 'what ifs and if onlys' this was life now and it was about how I could respond to and manage these unexpected circumstances in my life.

I had turned a major corner and found that I could laugh again, just like I had read about in the 'thought for the day' booklet and I began to see hope in the distance and in fact began to see with my inner eye that there was light at the entrance to my emotional dark cave and *also there were treasure chests as well, which still remained unopened.* One day I may have the courage to open them and see what lay inside for me, for Andrew, for us as a family and perhaps for others too. At least this is what I began to imagine. Our creative imagination can be a powerful tool in influencing our mood and as I began to improve in my emotional state as I spoke the words of forgiveness and began to change my focus.

For now, I had found a little joy in my darkness. I began to believe again that life would be worth living, I began to focus on the good things each day. I began to be thankful for all the things I did have, learning to have 'an attitude of gratitude' as I did have much to be thankful for, having a family, a home, employment, friends, transport, good services which did bring support and so the list went on.

When Julie was 16 years old, she and I went with our friends Paul and Christine Cocking to visit a programme in Guatemala, Central America. We sponsored a little boy and had the chance to be part of a team going out to visit them. These Guatemalan people are incredibly poor, living in little mud houses and came to the feeding programme which gave them a good meal, some education, dental, medical and spiritual input into their little lives. We visited the Doctor's surgery and he had such a small amount of medical equipment and medicines. I again was in tears as I thought of Andrew and all the services and supports that were in place to help him in his education and health. My mind was starting to become much clearer, in spite of this tragedy of Andrew's medical condition, I did in fact have lots to be thankful for in my life.

My brother gave me a book around that time written by two American Psychologists "Happiness is a Choice" by Minirth & Mier. Over half a million copies had been sold and I found it to be a useful study book in my recovery to wholeness and acceptance. I now understood, thanks to the Psychologist and to Carol Angus, my friend and Health Visitor, she explained to me that I had been going through bereavement and loss. I was now starting to come to terms with the massive change in my son. This gave me insight into the major life change I was facing and helping me to realise that I no longer had the son I thought I had. I began to feel more hopeful, the binding ropes of negative emotions no longer bound around me and I felt lighter, not so heavy, weary and fearful, but brighter, lighter and clearer in my thinking and my emotions.

It was however a very major loss to accept in our lives. There were many losses: a loss of developmental milestones for our little boy, which the average child makes automatically, as they grow and develop, but not so for Andrew. His intellectual and cognitive functioning was impaired and was functioning in some ways as a four year old. There was also a loss of peer friendships and social interaction. He did not understand how to make friends so reverted into himself and a sense of social isolation. Every person requires some social interaction in order to be fully functional and this had to be engineered for Andrew. It felt like no-one reached out to him to be his friend which was incredibly painful to observe his isolation. There was also a major loss of independence as he required to have a supporter with him wherever he went due to the complexity of his epilepsy and lack of awareness of safety issues.

Every parent has hopes, dreams and aspirations for their children. I was experiencing the loss of all the possible dreams and aspirations I had for him and his future. It was as if the future dreams for Andrew's life had crashed to the floor and lay shattered in a scattered unsightly heap. I had to learn to lay them down in an orderly fashion and accept who Andrew was now, as a young man growing up with limited mental ability. This explained the millions of tears and all the dark emotions. I now understood why I had grieved so deeply for all these losses and for all these expectations which were not met and probably would never be met. It began to make sense to me and I became much more self-aware of why I felt the way I did.

I do believe that as we have an increased understanding of self-awareness, this enables us to recognise emotions and learn to analyse why we feel what we feel and then choose our emotional responses to a given situation. When negative emotions now come my way, I have an internal dialogue with myself about what I am feeling, recognising the source and then deciding how I want to emotionally respond in the situation.

It was now time to move forward and come to some kind of closure on this intense grief and depression. I did not want to live in that dark cave any longer. There is a quote which says *'Life is like a coin it can only be spent once'*. I wanted to make each day count, so I now turned the corner into acceptance. I read in a booklet about the sad circumstances which we face in our lives and the challenge was about them making us *'Bitter or Better'*.

I made the decision - *I wanted to be better.*

There are no shortcuts
to any place worth going

5.   Moving south

School was changing. The secure, precious, special unit was closing as all children would be included in the mainstream class. Andrew needed one to one support to continue his education meaningfully or in a secure and safe environment, but where was his place, where did he fit?

One day when we were visiting our old caravan at Lossiemouth for the week-end, I saw a TV programme about epilepsy. St Piers School in Lingfield, Surrey was being filmed and it was highlighting the school being involved in Lamotrigine trials which was a new anti-convulsant medication and they were also piloting work with the video telemetry system. This is a system where the Electroencephalogram (EEG) is also synchronised with a video camera. When a seizure is occurring, the body movements can also be observed at the same time on the TV screen. I was totally engaged with this programme and my immediate thought was *"I must take Andrew there, as they are truly Leaders in their field"*.

We had managed to scrape together enough money to purchase this old static caravan at Seatown, Lossiemouth and we had lots of week-ends as well as our annual holiday there. It was a little paradise overlooking the numerous sand dunes and out to the sea. Often it was cold, wet and windy but that did not deter us......we all donned our wellingtons and raincoats and off we would go to explore the beach and spend the pocket money on itsy bitsy treasures from the local shop. A portable TV was rigged up, which was powered off a 12 volt battery and we watched an occasional programme in the inclement weather.

On our return from that Lossiemouth holiday, I wrote to St Piers School to ask about the possibility of Andrew being assessed. The Medical Director rang me to discuss Andrew's condition. After a long conversation, we agreed that the best route forward would be for us to have a visit to St Piers and talk with the Medical Director then take it from there. We all went down for a visit and my sister Elizabeth also accompanied us, as she was a Paediatric Nurse and we felt that her opinion was also very important to us.

St. Piers is set in the middle of lush suburban countryside and as you enter the little village, there are squirrels darting up and down the huge oak trees, a sense of spaciousness, warmth and acceptance pervades the air. We met with the Medical Director and at the conclusion of our visit it seemed that it would be appropriate for Andrew to be assessed at St. Piers as his condition met their criteria. However the assessment was not a few days, as I had hoped, but was a minimum of six months! This was a big shock to me as it would mean a residential placement, Andrew leaving home from the north of Scotland and going down to the south of England. So this was another blow, I hadn't anticipated this would be the case. I had expected to go with Andrew for a few days assessment, now I had to face yet another big hurdle of my little nine year old lad leaving home. This also meant that we had to ask the Highland Council and Health Board to fund Andrew's residential place for him to attend St Piers School.

On our return, I rang a senior officer in the Highland Council regarding the possibility of Andrew having the placement at St Piers and he said to me *"Who do you think you are? There are many children in Highland*

Region with epilepsy". He did not realise that Andrew was diagnosed with Lennox Gastaut Syndrome Epilepsy which is the most severe type and accounts for 1% of all epilepsy cases!

I came off the phone absolutely reeling from his raw, hierarchal, paternalistic response, feeling put down and disempowered by his superior reply, but determined within myself, at that moment, that I would not be daunted by bureaucracy and decided that I would expect favour with the key professionals. I wrote to the Head Teacher, Parent School Council, Area Education Officer and Highland Health Service with our request. Everyone told us that we would not get the funding, as budgets were tight......I always find it interesting how quick people are to respond with the negatives rather than the encouragements, however I held firm in my resolve and passionately hoped during these days that we would secure the best for Andrew.

The important day arrived when a Review was being convened to discuss Andrew's case. I was very nervous and felt hugely emotional, wanting the best for Andrew, yet my heart breaking at the thought of sending my nine year old son to the south of England. George managed to get time off work and attend that Review, as did my sister Elizabeth, as our 'named person' since she could also give a health perspective. There was much discussion around the table with various professionals and the school doctor, a lady who commanded high respect, recognised that, the equipment, knowledge and expertise which St. Piers had, was not equalled in Scotland. So it was agreed that the placement would be funded jointly by Health and Education Departments. This was a major triumph for me, after the treatment I had received from the senior Highland Council officer. It also taught me a very important lesson, not to give up at the first hurdle, to be persistent, to be assertive and not aggressive, to keep asking and go through the correct channels, playing by the rules of the game and we won.

The English school term began in September, so Andrew returned to our local school for a few weeks until he was due to move south. It was not the most meaningful time for him and we felt that this English placement was indeed fortuitous. Placing Andrew into the mainstream class did not work as he really needed 1:1 support. Children who were in Primary 5 were now much more capable and independent, but Andrew needed constant support, reminding and coaching him to stay on task. In fact one day Andrew came home from school at lunch time and the school staff were not aware of it. Fortunately I was at home at the time and I had rather a lot to say to the Head Teacher about 'so called inclusion' that day!

The day dawned for Andrew to leave home and take the trip down to London and out to Lingfield where St Piers school was located. Andrew and George travelled down in the aeroplane from Inverness to London. George was going to Honduras in Central America on a missionary trip for four weeks, so it was convenient to plan this en route. As I looked out of my patio door that very early Monday morning and saw the London plane circle to go south, I noticed the aeroplane lights in the grey, dawning sky, which reminded me of that light and hope that I had to cling on to during these school terms of separation. Not only had my son gone to the bottom of England, but my husband had gone away abroad for a month as well. His job entailed working at various locations across Highland in different BT Radio Stations, so he was only home at week-ends. He needed time to get away and think and process his thoughts. I had to carry on with all the normal caring responsibilities of my two children, my mother and my brother. My heart was so sad and tearful at the separation, but I wanted the best for Andrew and was focussed on the outcome that this was the top school in UK for children with complex epilepsy and if anyone can help him – they can. This thought kept me positive, that I was doing my very best for my son.

Andrew was placed in a house called 'Ruston'. It was a lovely old house, which had approximately ten other boys, all of whom had complex epilepsy and learning difficulties. The junior school was separate from the secondary school and there was a swimming pool, adventure play area, various other small buildings to play snooker and other leisure activities. It was truly a beautiful place filled with love, care, kindness and seeking to reach each child's potential.

We saw Andrew every three weeks, either flying down to visit or he was coming back home for mid term. Telephone calls, cards, little presents were constantly winging their way on surface mail. My sister-in-law Isobel and her friend Christine also visited Andrew as did my sister Elizabeth. Some people sent cards and gifts too which was greatly appreciated. The little Baptist Church in Dormansland welcomed Andrew and one couple regularly collected him each week for the Sunday service, which was really kind of them and gave us a feeling of moral support.

Time passed slowly and Andrew appeared to be very much at home in this environment with many others like himself. There were 220 pupils on site and the curriculum was tailored to his needs and intensive EEG monitoring was a regular feature for many children. They did twenty four hour readings with a mobile fob attached to the collar of his shirt, gathering all the brain wave data. The staff at the school were dedicated to this cause and were true professionals in their field.

When full assessments had been completed over the six months, we were invited down for a Review at St. Piers. The Medical Director explained to us that the EEG interpretations indicated that Andrew was having *five thousand subtle seizures in a twenty four hour period*! This meant that his little life was like watching a video tape of pieces cut out every few seconds and trying to make sense of the story. He also said that oftentimes, children in this category often had severe behavioural problems, so we were thankful that this had not been a major challenge to us at that time. He complimented our parenting skills. We always felt it important to treat both children the same in learning how to behave and respect adults. We now had a clear prognosis of his condition and a very impressive assessment of every possible aspect to his life. This positive feedback our resolve to rigorously pursue Andrew's social skills in order that we could take him into any social situation.

The placement was extended to finish that school year, so the total placement was nine months and Andrew was due to return home. I wanted to have a little celebration to mark the importance of the occasion. I hired a small bouncy castle and had the BBQ smoking, various garden toys and seats were out in our back garden, music playing and even the sun was shining! We had invited several of our friends round for the occasion to welcome Andrew home. They all came, with lovely little gifts for Andrew, which was so kind, but the most important gift was missing.......the friendship of other children.

Only the adults came, but without their children. Exclusion again. It felt like a bitter sweet pill, our friends came but didn't bring their children, so Andrew played alone on the bouncy castle. Did they not understand or appreciate that I wanted Andrew to be included with other children? Oh how my heart deeply ached again on this return. Although I had moved from the black cave of depression, I still had a long journey ahead.

Good friends are good for your health

6.   The Silent Doorbell

We were ready for change.   Andrew was happily established back home in the Scottish Highlands and ready to start his new school – Drummond Special School in Inverness. We were ready for it too, having seen him so happy with his peers at St Piers School, we knew he belonged in this special educational environment with children who were like him and had similar behaviours, abilities and responses.

On the first day he was due to go to the school, the doorbell rang and a white taxi was waiting in the driveway. A friendly lady introduced herself, telling me she was the transport escort and would be accompanying Andrew to school. I spent a few minutes explaining the epilepsy to her and she assured me that *'he would be safe in her hands'* and they were off, waving with enthusiasm. I really hoped she had been briefed on epilepsy, but didn't really know. I had reservations, after all Andrew regularly had seizures in the morning and if he hadn't had one at breakfast time, he could have en route to school. I didn't feel too confident about the friendly lady going off with him. The day passed uneventfully and Andrew returned back home again at 3.15pm and the door closed.

Andrew quickly settled into special school and was happy going off each day in the taxi. He had a bubbly, friendly and understanding teacher who seemed to reach for the children's full potential, in spite of their disabilities, which was really good. We received positive reports in the daily notebook which went back and forth to the school. This was a very useful communication tool, especially if your child can't relay any information back about their day. It also meant that it was a *'two way street'* as we always wrote in any relevant information which reflected home life about what Andrew had done or where we had gone on outings.

The children in our street were also back in school, but of course they were going to the local primary school. The delights of our large back garden with swings and other garden toys held no more interest for the local children. Their own levels of independence were being fulfilled by going up to the village play park and further afield. They were now outgrowing Andrew's usefulness as they were now growing up, becoming more independent and getting more personal freedom.

Our home was a comfortable, spacious five bed roomed bungalow. This house was the second house we had built, which was in the village of Smithton, Inverness. We built a five bed roomed house to accommodate my Mother, so it was much more spacious and now we also had a dining room, where I taught all my piano pupils. The house was well furnished and Andrew had his own bedroom, which had plenty of space to play. He had lots of interesting toys and activities to keep him amused and was in fact quite resourceful in using his time.

I always encouraged our children to have *meaningful and purposeful play,* I did not allow the word 'bored' to be used as there were always lots of interesting things to do and also things that did not cost money. We always watched 'Blue Peter' the children's TV programme in these days and then we would make the crafty items which they demonstrated out of cornflakes boxes etc. In fact my daughter Julie, now married with her own family stills keeps the 'treasure box' we made together when she was 10 years old. I ensured that our children had lots of indoor and outdoor play experiences, playing lots of physical games which keeps them fit and active, also teaches turn taking and problem solving activities, learning how things work.

On Saturdays we would have a family outing and often go rambling up the woods at Clava Cairns a few miles out of Inverness, where there were lots of streams and the children loved paddling with their wellingtons and gathering sticks and stones. We would always have a simple picnic with us and sit on the grass making up songs. Although Andrew had this condition of complex epilepsy, we saw it as a high priority for him to join all these activities, always ensuring his safety.

Misty the dog was integral to all these trips and she loved chasing around the woods and running after the stick which brought great delight to Andrew. He loved his dog and would cuddle her tight – we always felt he had a very special relationship with the dog. So, it has been interesting to note that as Andrew grew up, he had a great affinity with animals and was always resourceful at amusing himself, as that was the family ethos living our lives with meaning, enjoyment and fulfilment.

During the summer holidays, I was always there for the children, as I did not teach piano in the school holidays and we would have lots of interesting things to do together. We would all bake together or make models on wet days, play outdoor games and do rambles on dry days. When the circus came to town we would always enjoy an afternoon visit and when we returned home would try to get Misty the dog to do the tricks they did at the circus but she would not obey our efforts!! We would take a plank of wood and put it on a large concrete block and tempt her with a doggie sweet but she would always run round it rather than run on it.....our attempts at being a circus performer were not very fine tuned.

I usually read a book to the children during the summer holidays and each day I would read a chapter to them. I think this is such an important activity as it really encourages imagination when listening to the story. In fact often we would sit out in the garden to do the story time and sometimes other kids wanted to join in our little group. Julie loves to recount the story of me making chips late evening, then wrapping them in greaseproof paper and newspaper then handing them out to all the children through kitchen window. The kids all pretended that it was a chip shop!

Socialisation is so important in all of our lives. We are all created to relate with other human beings. So much is learned from human relationships, our values, social codes of behaviour, learning skills and developing language, expressing emotions, enjoying new experiences which shape us. In fact I have done lots of work with older people and a major key issue is social isolation which often initiates depression. When we socialise together, this usually enhances the mood. Social isolation is a major factor in the learning disability world and it is so important to ensure that people with learning disabilities have adequate opportunities to socialise in meaningful ways.

I felt it was so important for Andrew to have some opportunities to play and interact with his peers, in order to utilise that social development, through play and leisure. I didn't want him out the house every night, but just some play time with peers, out with school hours. After all, it's quite normal for children to be out playing with their friends. However, I had difficulty finding any clubs he could join. The main one was the Smithton Free Church who ran a Monday club for primary children where they did lots of singing and taught a bible story. They were happy to have Andrew join the club and he greatly enjoyed these times. How I deeply appreciated their willingness to include him and indeed have been indebted to them throughout the years for many other supports they have shown to me in my community project development work.

Our home was always filled with music. I grew up with music. My brother, sister and myself all play piano. My own home always had music playing, if I wasn't playing music myself, Julie would be playing her piano or trumpet. However, I began to recognise an *'eerie accompaniment'* which had crept into my home:

The silent doorbell

Yes, the doorbell had stopped ringing.

No longer were there children on my front step looking up to me saying, *"Is Andrew coming out to play?"* Only very occasionally would Sean or James call, two faithful friends from the street, but soon they too stopped calling as they were gaining more independence and Andrew was developing the habit of staying home and was becoming socially isolated - *and we were too.* It was becoming too great a risk for Andrew to be playing along at the play park climbing bars in the street as one day he had a seizure when playing there.

Another day Andrew was playing on his bike in our driveway and a little lad came up to the gate. He shouted to Andrew *"You're a Drummond".* This of course referring to the special school he attended – a lovely school where staff cared for their physical needs and educated them as far as their limited potentials would allow. Truly a place which was a haven of love, care, understanding, patience, commitment and filled with *'going the extra mile'* staff. How could this child say with such stigma and strength *"You're a Drummond"?* I felt saddened, confused and hurt that a child would have this perception. Is this how people perceive those with learning difficulties? Do they treat them with disrespect rather than kindness?

My heart was sad that day as I mused on this comment. The normal interaction which happens between families when children are school friends, was non-existent in our home. Somehow I had to *'make that doorbell ring again'* not only for our son, but perhaps too, for all the other 'Andrews'. I asked myself over and over, *"how did other parents feel, did they have silent doorbells too, how could I meet them"?*

When my daughter Julie was growing up through her childhood, she had lots of little friends who came to her birthdays and she to them. They played in each other's gardens and she went to little clubs and groups. Alas, there appeared to be nothing like that for Andrew. He couldn't follow the rules of games so how could he meaningfully participate? The gap got wider and wider as he reached the years of 9yrs 10yrs and 11yrs, I saw this as a journey of *progressive grief*, where he did not reach the developmental milestones and there were more and more social situations, where Andrew was excluded and could not meaningfully participate. Where did he fit? Where was his special place in society?

I always loved going to the Drummond School sports day and the annual concerts. At these occasions, every child and teenager in the school was included in some way.

There I saw youngsters who were much more severely disabled than Andrew and they had their place, their part, their little bit that they could do. Sport's day actually brought much laughter as kids ran in wrong directions or collected the beanbag prematurely or whatever, but all of us parents cheered them on none the less – they were all winners!

Andrew being a pupil in Drummond School gave me that sense of him *belonging* to this unique group of children who had special needs but were friends together at school, at least this was somewhere, in the world where he belonged. However, what about out of school hours, where did he belong? In fact where did I belong as his Mother? All my friend's children were flourishing, developing, being educated, had little friends, finding hobbies and interests for themselves, but what could I say about Andrew, very little. There was a feeling of displacement, not being fully connected somehow. It's like being the onlooker, in the background, not in the forefront or the heart of things. Yes it felt displaced and disconnected. Andrew was isolated when we went to church as the children played with their friends but he was always alone. How my heart ached as I chatted to friends and watched out the corner of my eye, seeing him so Alone. Alone. Alone.

I felt that I had to start something for Andrew and all the other 'Andrews' that I hadn't yet met. How could I do it? What would I do? It was a burning desire within me to DO SOMETHING instead of ongoing moping about the isolation and displacement. I had lots of experience working with children and young people, doing all kinds of activities, clubs and youth camps, but I had no experience of disability. Only what I had learned through Andrew. I had also gleaned some valuable information from CHIP –

Children in the Highlands Information Point. They were a little charity who gave information to parents and professionals. The lady who ran the service was so kind, compassionate and understanding about my issues and it helped me process the fact that there were many others out there in similar circumstances.

Where could I start I wondered?   How could I get to know all these other children who went off in a taxi at 9am and returned at 3.15pm then, their doors closed too.

I needed to find a way through this loneliness.

After all, I now had new hope and light was shining in that dark cave, I had to use it, not just for myself, but for others. I didn't want to go back to the blackness, I wanted to go towards the light. I had to pursue action – and I did!

Attitude is a decision

7.   Social Supporters

I reflected on how I could make that doorbell ring again and decided to talk with the Head Teacher of the special school, so I rang the school and asked for a meeting with the Head Teacher. Although the Head had a very busy job, he took the time to listen to my story and I said to him that perhaps we could start a 'Support Group' of some kind. He encouraged me to take this step and suggested that we could have a public meeting in the school and discuss it as a possibility. The school board was well established and they had some public information to share with the parents, so a short discussion followed at the end of the meeting regarding my suggestion of setting up a parent support group.

Several parents showed interest and I was voted in as Chairperson to start off this new group 'Drummond Parents Support Group'. The group began to meet on a monthly basis. We shared our backgrounds, problems, dreams and aspirations. Guest speakers would sometimes come along and give us valuable information, they were usually Health Professionals. We shared information with each other and discovered that many of us were not receiving the benefits which we were entitled to, nor had community care assessments, nor were receiving respite services. We decided to have some action and start asking for our rights!

We ran occasional coffee mornings on Saturdays and bric a brac was sold, making £25 - £30 to help with any running costs. These were held in Drummond Special School and we appreciated the support of the Head Teacher and some staff on these occasions. They were happy times when we began to meet a wider group of parents. Everyone was there, with their disabled child and it helped us to realise that we were not alone, but there were many families all experiencing common issues, even although a wide range of disability was represented.

We all had a common issue – we all had "silent door bells". Yes we all knew what it was like at 3.15pm when the taxi dropped off our child and the door closed with no friends ringing the bell wanting to play with our child. We all knew what it was like during the long summer holidays when our child had nowhere to go and no-one to play with, while the other siblings had lots of interesting friends and activities. However, now we were starting to get connected to each other and the isolation was just beginning to diminish, we were discovering and creating a place of belonging to each other.

Although I felt this deep sense of isolation, much of it was an inner, emotional isolation. The importance of a supportive family is a key ingredient to the disability journey. My husband always took an active role in fatherhood and played an integral part to the roles and responsibilities, which were thrust upon us.

Our daughter Julie was most accepting throughout these developmental years and loved her brother. As she grew older she was happy to child mind on many, many occasions which I deeply appreciated. I recall many times during the long school holidays when I would ask Julie to child mind for a couple of hours and I would go off in the car and sit by the harbour in Avoch or out to Arderseir and I would write poetry, as it was a creative outlet for me instead of always grieving and this past time produced a little poetry book which reflected thoughts of the day's culture. However it was important that Julie had her life to live too and we always ensured that her desires were heard and met as appropriate. During her teenage years,

73

we would go off on 'girlie trips', travelling to various locations enjoying mother and daughter time together.

I was in the fortunate position of having an understanding family. My mother was living with us and my sister lived nearby. Andrew had enjoyed many teas at Auntie Elizabeth's house, which was always a highlight for him. She always went the extra mile in taking him a trip to Nairn beach or some other place of interest. They would sometimes have tea out and then come home and have fun with board games – even although Andrew could not follow the rules of the game. She had a great sense of humour and if Andrew became un-cooperative in any way, she would speak to the 'furry monkey' and tell him to behave! This always evoked a great thunder of laughter from Andrew and brought him out of his little moods. She always had some kinds of treat or 'picnic' as she called it, during the evening when they played or watched a special programme or dvd on the TV. Elizabeth took Andrew on many occasions and provided a welcome respite for us – especially during the teenage years, for which we were very grateful.

My brother mainly lived in Ireland but had a good rapport with Andrew when he came to visit. They enjoyed musical times at the piano where Andrew would sing along and bang away on his guitar while Charles played the piano by ear with all his fascinating harmonic progressions of chords. I often used to ask him "What chord was that?" but he could never tell me as he played mainly by ear and didn't know the names of the chords. Although I could play piano by ear too, I always played by thinking about the chord progressions and what the names of the chords were, this was due to my classical music training. He would also play ball in the garden and go walks to the local village shop which encouraged Andrew to make a

Newborn Andrew
with sister Julie

Andrew's 4th birthday

Andrew's first day at
Smithton school

Andrew at St Piers School
in Lingfield, Surrey

Family Day out   Andrew loves horses

Andrew working
at Glachbeg Croft

Family Get Together
at Kirriemuir

Enjoying the snow
with sister Julie

Julie and Michael's
wedding in Dundee

Andrew moving into
his own home
9th April 2011

The Gift of Family

choice as to what kind of crisps would it be today, as choices were always a big challenge to Andrew and the challenge to me was waiting on him making the choice – which could take a few minutes!

My mother in law, Gran Normington and sister in law Isobel lived in Glasgow and were always very supportive of our situation and they did not show any difference in their love and acceptance of Andrew. When they visited us, Isobel and her friend Christine, would often take the children out for all kinds of interesting trips and treats to various places of interest and see animal farms, children's museums and special family interest events. They always showered them with special little gifts from these occasions which always brought great delight to show off on their return.

I was aware that Andrew was growing up, his peers now being independent to an extent, but my life constantly had the 'caring tie' attached to it. If I wanted to go anywhere, I always had to consider care for Andrew – who would be there for him. My piano pupils came for their lessons from 3.30pm onwards three nights per week and Andrew really needed someone there looking out for him while I was teaching.

A good friend called Chris Lafferty offered to take Andrew a session per week after school. She collected him and he enjoyed being at her home interacting with the three members of her family. Just the act of offering to help, meant so much, apart from the effort, sacrifice of time on her behalf, also the acceptance in dealing with seizures or behavioural issues was so supportive to me. Her husband Joe had stayed with us for a period of time when he was moving job to Inverness and Joe had a real connection with Andrew too, yet he himself is a deep academic thinker. One day Andrew was watching for Joe coming home and ran out to meet him at his car saying "I've opened the door for you". Joe, as usual, was accepting and affirming, thanking Andrew for his kindness. So simple yet so profound, demonstrating open acceptance of Andrew's limited intellect. This is such a significant memory as Andrew's verbal communication was extremely limited and it was a precious moment when he spoke these simple words to Joe.

Carol and Eddie Angus were always interested in Andrew and our family life. In fact Eddie had worked at St Piers School as a young man and was instrumental in supporting our decision to send Andrew there for assessment. They would buy the most beautiful and classic gifts for Andrew, usually impeccably wrapped with an idyllic card. Everything was always done to an excellent standard. Carol was a Health Visitor and she provided me with important information about benefits and helped me in my journey of grief and loss.

Christine, Eddie and Adam Lyle shared many holidays with us. Their son also had some special needs, being on the autistic spectrum and a friendship was formed with the two lads even although there is seven years between them. This friendship had a real benefit to all of us and we have supported each other through the many ups and downs of disability over the years even although they live in the south of England.

The Macintosh family have been longstanding friends too. Chris and Edith have lived in different Scottish locations, but always kept in touch and fully accepted Andrew for who he is when we visited together. We have spent many great times together as families and their friendship is treasured.

As young families we sometimes shared days out on a Saturday to local beaches such as Nairn or Rosemarkie and we would collect shells and take them home as treasures to make models or pictures. We would always take a picnic in these days as money was tight and that was all part of the fun, running around playing games then being rewarded by all the sandwiches and treats which came out of the Tupperware containers. I used to be a Tupperware Representative and my kitchen cupboards had rather a lot of these plastic containers. One minister friend said to me *"My wife had a Tupperware party with you and now the whole church has Tupperware in their cupboards!"*

Martin and Ruth Baldwin have been great supportive friends to us too and although much of their time has been spent abroad doing humanitarian work and developing businesses for the poorest of the poor in a remote part of Guatemala in Central America. They have helped and supported us on their return to UK where we have spent lots of happy week-ends and holiday breaks enjoying long discussions about some of the big questions in life. These conversations were stimulating and supportive, as dialogue on difficult subjects can often bring clarity to our thinking and helps us in our coping strategies with demanding situations in our lives.

Paul and Christine Cocking have also been very good friends, always interested in our life journey and bringing us words of encouragement, just when we needed it. We have also shared lots of good times with them and in fact went with them on their first trip to Guatemala in 1994 as they are responsible for some large Humanitarian Projects providing feeding programmes for children. George would often meet Paul and I would meet Christine separately for lunch and chat through some of our challenges. We often met together as couples and shared our stories of life together over a pleasant meal.

'Girlie Friends' were important to me as well, where we could meet for coffee and just 'share life together'. Everyone has their own story to tell and the difficulties which face them. Mairi Beaton, the lady who came on the SNAP Board, then became SNAP Project Manager became a regular friend to swap stories and support each other. I remember when I first met Mairi as she came along to an AGM for our SNAP organisation and was very interested in the project. She has a lovely family and one of her daughters has a disability. When running any voluntary sector organisation, getting keen volunteers with valuable skills is like gold, so we invited Mairi to come on to the committee and she became a long term friend and highly valuable champion of the organisation. To date she has given ten years of her life to SNAP.

My friend Liz Syred became my charity partner in developing our confidence building programme called 'Reaching High' and latterly became a close friend and supporter as we went through the dark patches of transition. How I have appreciated being able to share ongoing developments in my later part of my life with Liz and also enjoy working with her in an entrepreneurial manner. She has been a very supportive and understanding friend. She has had her fair share of life's challenges to go through as well and having that breadth of relationship is so important to keep a balanced view in life, as there is a real danger of polarisation when coping with disability and not appreciate the diversity of hardship which many other people face in their lives.

Karen and Robbie Halkett were always so kind to Andrew and including him in every way possible and so supportive sending us a beautiful bouquet of flowers on the day Andrew moved into his own house, which was such a gesture of love, kindness and care at such a sensitive passage in our lives. They frequently invited us round at Hogmanay to share that special time of the 'New Year Bells' together and we so appreciated this inclusion. They often gave him gifts at church and ensured he was included in family events and prize giving occasions, even although he was an adult, he really enjoyed these gestures.

I was so grateful for faithful, loyal, interested and supportive friendships and family. This enabled and supported me and gave me the courage and moral support to continue in my caring role and latterly my lobbying role as well. If you are a parent of a child with a disability, I would encourage you to have friends who 'know *what it's like to have a disabled child'* but also to keep a range of friendships within your life. The gift of friendship is one of the most special gifts in life and it is something which we must cherish and work at to keep these special relationships alive. Being in circles of friendship bring enrichment and support to our life journey.

Although Andrew was accepted within the church we previously attended, sadly he was not allowed to participate in the youth group in his early teenage years. This deeply hurt and saddened me - that he could not be included - the answer was just "no". How awful it felt to be on the outside and 'not fitting the mould' yet church is supposed to be a big happy family together? I must say that left big questions in my head. However, when the leadership of the youth group changed over to our friends Iain and Liz Mackenzie, they welcomed him in to the group with no problem whatever. The McKenzie family were also such good friends. Always accepting, believing, understanding and willing to help out where possible and appropriate. Andrew often had times at their home and in fact when I travelled abroad to Hong Kong and Singapore with an American lady for four weeks, Liz cared for Andrew on numerous occasions to make that trip possible. Her husband Iain was a social worker and immensely supportive, as was his son Simon who just took Andrew in his stride. So it's important to remember the good memories and release the bad ones!

As the Drummond Parent Support Group developed, I began to ask lots of questions. I discovered that there was a large support network out in society which had never touched my life.......the Voluntary Sector. This was a new term to me, who and what was the Voluntary Sector? I heard about a wide range of organisations which were charitable, not for profit organisations working within the field of leisure, social welfare and many other fields of interest, so this was the Voluntary Sector.

Crossroads was a Voluntary Organisation who provide *care at home.* I realised that in order to receive community care, I had to contact Social Work Services. This was a really big hurdle for me as I always associated Social Work with dysfunctional families and that wasn't us! However, I had to accept that if I wanted support for Andrew and also for my mother, by this time she was becoming really frail, I had to go through the Social Work route. The Social Worker came to my house and did her assessment, which took a fair amount of time, endless questions, going over Andrew's story again and also having to give all the information about my mother and her needs as she became more dependant and frail. It felt such an invasion into our personal lives.

I recall on one occasion when the social worker had a look around the house and commented that Andrew had a double bed. I felt her comment was demanding some kind of answer...The reason that Andrew slept in a double bed was that he frequently had nocturnal seizures and had often fallen out the single bed in the night and we got him a double instead. In fact back in the early 20th century they had 'epilepsy beds' which were virtually mattresses on the floor as their clients often fell out of bed in the night with nocturnal seizures.

It felt like our lives were on view in the public domain, even although we had nothing to hide, it was an enormous invasion into our privacy. However, in order to access the respite services, these were the hoops that we had to jump through to meet the criteria.

We began to receive care for both Andrew and my ageing mother from Crossroads. This was a huge bonus as it was a flexible service and we booked the care when we needed it. We were greatly appreciative of this service being given to us. Interestingly enough, the Social Worker told us that when we receive respite, this is *a break* for us, where we should be having time off and a bottle of wine. Instead, we were always at church meetings. On reflection, she was right! We certainly needed a real break from everything. We were so highly committed people and dedicated to the cause that we rarely allowed ourselves any indulgence of having time off. This was an important lesson to learn that we needed to learn to 'chill out' when we got the chance.

I recognised that I needed to get connected much more widely in order to develop a new project with our disabled children in our group. I couldn't develop ideas alone or only with the existing group of parents. It was imperative to find out how the system worked and play the big game by the big rules. The game and the rules of the Voluntary Sector were all new to me, but I was open to learn and found out that I was a quick learner! Having a strong network of social support from a variety of sources is crucial to our emotional well being, whatever our circumstances and I am most grateful for all the family, friends and colleagues who have given valuable input into our lives.

All these different kinds of support gave me a new strength and deep resilience for this journey of disability. I had looked so much to the church for my support and realised that I needed to find the *appropriate kind of support* and much of that relevant support was found in meeting with other parents and support organisations which knew in depth about disability issues.

My commitments and priorities began to change in my life. Instead of being immersed in church activities I became actively involved in community and learning who to connect with and how resources were secured through charitable means. This was also a new world to me and I became interconnected with lots of organisations and colleagues within the Voluntary and Statutory sectors.

As a result, I think some people misunderstood me when my priorities changed, but life had changed dramatically for me and I had to find my way through with the right support and information which would guide me through this new maze of community care. I think that it is so important to 'stay in the flow of life' and be open to the doors which open for us, as we can miss all important moments in our lives.

For me, this was a defining time of change, connection, priority, learning and relationships, so life was changing dramatically as I made new decisions about how I spent my time and used my skills in my life.

*It is better to light one small candle
than to curse the dark*

8.   A New Project

The Drummond Parents Support Group had successfully existed for at least six months. We continually discussed, our 'silent doorbells'. I was a strong advocate for starting a club of some kind and the parents all agreed in a consensus chorus. However, where could we start? We needed to get some key people on board to help us. My knowledge about Local Authority was extremely minimal, apart from the days when I worked in Civil Service as a Clerical Officer many years before. I decided to ask our close friend Iain McKenzie for advice. He was a Social Worker and did development work within the Voluntary Sector and sat on numerous committees, so I reckoned that he would 'know the ropes' and at least put me in the right direction.

His advice to me was, to convene a public meeting and invite parents and some key professionals from social work, health and community education. I already had some facilitation skills, since I often did public speaking, so was not too daunted by the idea. Iain knew the names of relevant professionals, so I duly invited them all along to the Spectrum Centre which is in the centre of Inverness. On the night in question, we had some input from Florence Williamson the local champion for Enable the national organisation for learning disability, also an NHS Speech and Language Therapist who mainly worked in the special school and the Area Social Work Manager with some of her colleagues. Several parents also attended and we discussed in small groups, the issue of play and socialisation for children with learning disabilities.

There was a unanimous agreement that evening that such a service was desperately needed in our town and everyone was most positive in encouraging a new club to be developed. The Area Social Work Manager was very supportive and gave lots of helpful advice encouraging us to meet with her and offered further support and resources. The Area Community Education Officer and the Community Education worker were also both very supportive towards the project and they offered the use of the Spectrum Centre for our club. They also gave us some really practical information for operating the club and keeping everyone safe.

SNAP (Special Needs Action Project) began. Our new project was born. We made up little fliers and put them out through the special school and on 19th November 1996 the first night of the SNAP Club began. It was a memorable night which I will never forget. We had very little resources of any kind. Our small amount of coffee morning money had not gone too far, but we bought what we could. I brought along a variety of games and CD player to have some background music, also brought my guitar to have a little sing along session. Jill Clunas a very committed parent to SNAP brought along colouring books and pens and toys etc. Although we did not have much in these days, we had something which could not be priced - We had each other and we felt connected and supported.

We all belonged to a unique club – families with *disabled* children. All ages, stages, conditions and ranges of physical and learning disabilities. In fact as I got to know Jill Clunas, I discovered that her son had the same condition as Andrew and we really connected with each other, sharing such a similar life journey. I knew about epilepsy but not about all these other complicated medical conditions and syndromes which many of the children had who attended the club. We all had to learn very fast about each other. I was only learning how to work a computer in those days and a friend was staying with us for a season, so she was very competent in administration and did lots of initial setting up of data bases and forms which was a great support.

The Spectrum Community Centre kindly gave us a free let in these days and the Community Education staff team were most supportive and helpful. It had lots of space and as the weeks went by, the numbers grew, as did the amount of equipment. Within three months we had fifty children with disabilities! This was quite a responsibility, to oversee and ensure safety at all times. Many of my friends came along and helped as volunteers, drivers and escorts. The parents all invited friends to help out as well and often some of the parents would stay for the evening, sitting around chatting and drinking tea.

There was lots of goodwill out in the community for the SNAP Club. People often approached us and offered to raise funds for certain items of equipment and our assets grew rapidly. Each week we brought down all the equipment – it was all stored in our garage and my husband spent each Thursday evening packing the vehicle then after work on Friday, a very quick meal and down to the Centre for 6.30pm to unpack and lay out the three large rooms, which we used for different activities.

There was a disco in the corner, tables with board games, play dough and colouring in, crafts and a snooker table. In the large hall there were some ride on toys and often organised games. The theatre provided a suitable environment for the projector which projected images on the wall in a circular motion. Some of the children who had more severe and profound needs just loved reclining on the big bean bags and enjoying the atmosphere.

It really wasn't that difficult to provide this simple play environment. We just needed plenty of helpers, mini bus drivers and escorts. Thankfully, many people were willing to help and some of them continued to help for years. Everyone loved their Friday night SNAP club and lots of new friendships were emerging as a result of the club. Young people were coming from secondary schools, using the club as a place to gain experience for their Duke of Edinburgh Award. Crossroads sent some workers for children who needed one to one support. Social Care workers also helped out with 1:1 support from Social Work Department. There was lots of partnership working happening through the SNAP Project.

Parents and children alike loved SNAP. They all wanted more as Friday night was not enough! What about the long seven weeks of summer holidays? Parents wanted something during that time as well. By this time, we were attracting some small grants into SNAP. I was learning about the importance of networking and accessing funding streams through various Trusts, which were appropriate to the disability sector. Initially, I was quite nervous completing these funding applications, but soon became quite competent as the money rolled into the account - that was the bit I really enjoyed, then we could spend it on more activities!

By this time, the Highland Cross had donated a brand new mini bus to SNAP which was absolutely wonderful. The Highland Cross had been doing marvellous fund raising for many years. There are 750 participants who run 20 miles from Kintail then cycle 30 miles and finish in Beauly. To date they have raised £3,215,190. When they phoned to say we had been successful with our bid, we were absolutely thrilled that they had believed in us, as this was a really big donation to such a small charity and

94

we were thrilled that they believed in us to give us a brand new mini bus. BBC Children in Need gave the first sizeable donation to fund a summer play scheme, which comprised of outings to various places of interest in our new shiny mini bus. It was successful, although like anything else, had its teething problems and parents were learning to become employers. Before we knew it, October holidays had arrived and parents wanted more and more.......

I had been working as a Private Piano Teacher for the previous ten years or so and was finding that SNAP was taking over my life. During the day, I attended endless meetings with all kinds of community groups and statutory agencies, gaining information and support. From 3.30pm onwards, I was teaching piano. Thursday and Friday nights were SNAP nights, the weeks were racing by!

I shall always be grateful to our friends Helen and Dave Zavaroni. Helen started childminding Andrew and also did various domestic household tasks. She was a fantastic worker and I was deeply grateful for all she did for us during those formative years of SNAP. Initially when I asked if she would be interested in helping me, she said that *'old folks were her thing'* but I must say she adapted well to Andrew's needs and did a wonderful job for us at home. Her husband Dave was a joiner and he made various items for SNAP. He made a lovely stand for kids to play with the railway set and also made a wooden ramp to enter the hall with the wheelchairs. Their support enabled George and I to work full time during that period and their input made it possible for me to develop the SNAP project and facilitate the growth and capacity of SNAP.

Donald McLeod, a Community Development Consultant, and also a personal mentor had done a Feasibility Study for us, funded by the local Inverness & Nairn Enterprise Company. This study was to consider the possibility of building a Special Needs Adventure Play Centre. His conclusion to that study was that our infrastructure was fragile and needed strengthening and capacity building to become more established. He advised us that the service comes first and the building second, or perhaps never, if local buildings could be utilised. That seemed a slightly disappointing outcome to me at the time, but I saw the wisdom of it as time progressed.

We received our first big donation of funding from the Mental Health Foundation in partnership with some local agencies. I had to take the important decision of giving up my beloved piano teaching and the Committee employed me as the SNAP Development Officer. I had loved teaching piano over the last decade but now I had to respond to the doors which were opening to me – an entirely new field of work. One of my adult piano pupils was retiring from his post an NHS Dentist and he decided to start teaching privately so that worked out very well, where he took on most of my pupils. This was a major milestone in my life as I had imagined that I would be teaching piano for the rest of my life. Herein lies a very important point about *'going with the flow'* in life. I had not planned that Andrew would be disabled, nor had I planned that I would start a big project in the Voluntary Sector, since I knew nothing of it, but was open to the card which life had dealt to me and went through the new doors which opened to me.

During this time I had begun a course of study in Social Care through Inverness College, which meant regular study hours to one and two o'clock in the morning, since I was also working full time, in fact often worked sixty SNAP hours per week, there was so much to be done, as we had begun to deliver After School Clubs by this time. Needless to say this had a huge impact upon my life, health and wellbeing. I was hugely overworking as the project was booming, but that in itself brought lots of work, plus studying and regularly burning the midnight oil reading and writing essays, plus running the home and caring etc. etc.

The SNAP office was based in our spare bedroom, so all SNAP telephone calls came through our personal home phone at all times of the day and evening. Many parents requiring moral support in their situations, some depressed, marital issues, financial hardship, lack of adapted housing, all kinds of issues. Funding was limited, so everything was done on a shoe string. Thankfully, I had an extremely tolerant husband, who supported and helped, contributing endless hours himself to SNAP business. If he hadn't been so supportive, it could have cost me my marriage. Thankfully, we had a Social Work Children's manager on our Committee and Social Work gave us the use of an office, so the pressure began to alleviate at home.

A huge leap had to be made, from £30 takings at a coffee morning to securing £70,000 funding in one year. That was rapid growth in the first year of 1997. The Area Education Officer, Social Work Manager and Health Development Officer were all very supportive and emphasised the absolute importance of capacity building. We were now responsible for large amounts of public money and required some professional skills to be represented on our Management Committee. A group of very keen and enthusiastic parents was a fantastic help and resource for the day to day decision making providing the play services. However recruiting and managing staff, monitoring and evaluation reports and financial monitoring and management was another matter. This was a painful time in the life of the organisation, but I was assured a 'normal' aspect of community development, as a small user group grows into a valuable Service Provider. Some relationships were fractured temporarily, although most were recovered in time.

I had to go 'head hunting' for these skills. Once again, I was immensely grateful to those who joined the team: My GP from our local health centre, a Hospital Manager, an Accountant, a Banker and a Lawyer who was also a parent. I was immensely grateful to these busy professional people who were willing to give up their time and use their business skills for our organisation. SNAP had become a company limited by guarantee by this time and we had to register with Companies House, the national authority for registered companies and have a Board of Directors file appropriate returns. Although we had to recruit people with business skills, we still retained parents on the Board also as their input was so important to the development of the operational services.

There were numerous press articles promoting SNAP which gained a public profile and attention within the Inverness community. Businesses and individuals continued to be supportive in raising funds and helping, but there was still, lots of work to do with the Local Authority as we required to reach a place of securing an ongoing 'service level agreement'.

I had a major learning curve ahead about negotiation.

*A diamond is a chunk of coal
that made good under pressure*

9. Getting Established

The Friday night SNAP club was now a regular feature and flourishing success. Parents wanted more and felt the sense of belonging to SNAP, which was fulfilling an important gap in the life of their family. Not only was there a benefit to the child, but to the parents and also to siblings. Families met with families and the sense of support for one another was dynamic, powerful and almost tangible. The isolation was diminishing, the network was building, people felt a sense of belonging and connectedness and also it was often a place where valuable information was shared between parents.

I continued to network, attend conferences and became involved with the Out of School Care Federation, which was a Highland umbrella body supporting the development of After School Clubs. They were very well informed about national standards for play and also relevant funding streams. SNAP became a member club and I focussed on drawing from their enthusiasm, expertise and resources. Latterly, I sat on their Management Board as Vice Chair.

We decided that it was time to visit some other projects and five visits were made: An adventure play centre in London; Barnardos Project in Dundee; PLAYPLUS services in Stirling; Scotland Yard Adventure Play Centre in Edinburgh and an Inclusive Play Centre in Glasgow. All of these visits were highly valuable to us as we developed our own services and we were most grateful to all the Project Officers who took the time to show us round and tell us about their service, each one delivering something quite different, but every service seeking to provide services for children with disabilities.

Children's Rights began to dominate the play agenda. It had been quite easy to obtain small funding grants to pilot services, but I discovered that sustainability was a totally different ball game! Funders would not fund a service which was perceived as a statutory duty of the Local Authority. I discovered that the Children (Scotland) Act 1995 Section 22 and 27 covered issues of Children in Need and stated:

"Each local authority must provide a range and level of services to:

> Safeguard and promote the welfare of children in its area who are 'in need'
> Promote the upbringing of children 'in need' by their families
> Must provide day care for children 'in need' aged 5 or less and after-school and holiday care for children ' in need'
> Services must be designed to minimise the effect of the disability on a disabled child
> Services must be designed to minimise the effect of the disability, of a child adversely affected by the disability of another family member
> Give children the opportunity to lead lives which are as normal as possible"

These were the legal rights of our children! How could we assert these rights? I had never been involved in politics. In fact, I was brought up in a strict religious family where we did not vote. So I had to begin learning about how the Highland Council worked – each local Councillor covering a particular land area. Needless to say, I rapidly made it my business to get to know my local Councillor. Not only did I get to know this Councillor, but the chair of Social Work and also the Chair of Culture and Leisure. Lots of questions were asked and I then had to locate who the lead officers were for children's services within the Highland Council. Sadly, children with disability were at the bottom of the political agenda.

Most resources were channelled to children in care and at risk. However, I argued that families could become 'at risk' if preventative measures were not in place to support parents in their endless caring for their disabled child. If these children had been born fifty years before, they would have been relegated to a life of institutionalism, yet there was an expectation that parents should 'just cope' especially if you had a husband, lived in a comfortable home, had a car and a job.

How sad that these assumptions were made. All people have emotional responses and coping mechanisms regardless of our social backgrounds and it is unreasonable to expect that those who are educated, economically active and live in quality housing do not need support. We all have limitations in our lives. Professionals who work in the special needs field, train to work at a competent level, but parents just have to muddle along, day in and day out. The issue of the child's welfare being of paramount importance, and also providing appropriate socialisation with their peers.

Fifty years before, many of these children who were in the SNAP Project would have been living in Craig Phadrig which was a specialist Residential Establishment on the outskirts of Inverness, but since Care in the Community came into vogue in 1990s everyone was transferred into the community and of course parents were expected to do all the caring themselves. However, the issue of respite and out of school support didn't seem to figure very highly at all on the political or social care agenda.

I became quite conversant about this topic of Children's Rights and opened many discussions with various Council Officers, asking their responses to the Local Authorities' duties in relation to the Children (Scotland) Act 1995 and was often brushed aside. It was an emotional roller coaster, having secured funding for piloting Play schemes and After School Clubs and now they could possibly fold, because of no funding? We had found the initial development and start up funding but wanted the Local Authority to provide the ongoing funding as part of their 'duty' according to the Children's Act.

How could this be on the Council's conscience, to see these 'category one' services, as they were called, stop when they were so valuable and important. Some mums said that SNAP *'kept them sane'.* Numerous meetings ensued with the Council Officials. In the early days of development, we had convened a conference, which was very well attended and one Councillor suggested that we should do a presentation to the full Highland Council in the Chamber. We had a long wait.....nine months it took to be on the agenda. Donald McLeod and myself gave a stirring presentation about Local Authority responsibilities and five parents came on at the end with large A1 pictures of each of their children – it was a very emotive moment in the chamber, when all the Councillors looked in silence, at our children who needed this precious service. The immediate response was resounding: *"Emotive presentation. We need to be supporting this work. These children need these services. The work of SNAP is commended."*

Lots of negotiation still had to be done with the Council Officers. They wanted to meet with our Board of Directors, who were all busy people doing highly professional jobs, but had to respond immediately when the Council set the day and time. The SNAP Board were seeking to negotiate a Service Level Agreement. This is an agreement that the Council would contract with SNAP to provide a statutory service on their behalf. Mairi Beaton, a parent Board Member gave a very significant amount of time and support to the cause and played a major role in negotiating this agreement. Subsequently, she became the SNAP manager. There was also a Manager in Social Work, who became the Social Inclusion Partnership Manager, was also very supportive of the cause, for which I was most grateful.

At last the Service Level Agreement was agreed. We could begin to relax now, as things were becoming somewhat established. Thankfully, this meant that a block of funding (around 55%) would be released each year from the Social Work Budget to contribute to the services. Childcare Partnership also contributed, as did other Trusts. We always charged fees to the parents, as we felt that people valued a service more when they are directly contributing and this satisfied all of our Funders.

The whole process was very draining. I had sixteen sessional staff and twenty five volunteers working with SNAP and the possibility of running out of funds was very scary indeed. I hoped for, longed for and expected favour with key people and am thankful today that these expectations were answered. As the SNAP Organisation had built in capacity and secured sustainable funding the need for training became increasingly apparent. Various organisations visited SNAP, often asking for advice and information. SNAP policies and procedures had been customised with the help of the Out of School Care Federation and now others wanted to copy from us. Expansion was now touching a wider geographical area.

The Mental Health Foundation (MHF) invited me to deliver a presentation at their Annual Conference in the Grosvenor Hotel, Edinburgh on 21st May 1999. Mairi Beaton, SNAP parent and Board Member accompanied me for moral support. I told the SNAP story and thanked MHF for believing in us – a little fragile, inexperienced group of parents, with a passionate vision to see social change for our disabled children and we did! Trusts can play such an important role in aiding community development at grassroots level making a dynamic difference in the life of a community.

I will never forget my final metaphor in describing the daffodil bulb which sits under the earth but after the harsh winter presses through with its triumphant sunshine yellow and this was what the Mental Health Foundation had done for us, enabling us to employ a full time Development Officer to establish the SNAP organisation and service. The long and loud applause which followed my speech reverberates in my memory as the Mental Health Foundation proudly acknowledged what their funds had achieved.

As I reflect on this aspect, I am so grateful to all Funders who invested in SNAP. Without them, the service could never have been developed. It is also true to say that without the dedication and commitment of many parents and volunteers, the service could never have been developed.

Everyone played their part.

Thank you to all of them.

*A pessimist sees the glass half empty,
an optimist sees it half full*

10. Next Steps

SNAP now had a firm foundation. Some sustainable funding was in place and regular staff were becoming increasingly competent and doing quality work. The premises used for the After School Clubs were at the kind permission of the Smithton Free church, who gave much support to the cause and very reasonable rent. This again was thanks to Donald McLeod, Community Development Consultant who connected me to the Church Hall. By this time we had secured money to have our own office which was situated above the garage premises in Smithton and very handy for the play services.

The church had a spacious hall adjacent to their sanctuary and the large tarmac car park was used as an outdoor playground. We asked the police to give us use of crowd control barriers which created an enclosed area for play. SNAP invested in heavy duty go karts and dual therapy bikes, as this encouraged the children with co-ordination difficulties to be regularly exercising in a play environment. The setting was not purpose built or the ideal place, but certainly has proved to be a suitable environment to provide these highly valuable play opportunities.

I always hoped that one day, SNAP would have their own purpose built play centre, but for now, I highly commend the church for their support, tolerance and understanding given to see the organisation, reach a full capacity service. The play service provides for 70 Inverness Families, all of whom would have 'silent doorbells' without SNAP. Latterly, the office and club moved into the new Drummond School which was purpose built.

Sharon Fraser was an applicant for a job on the first ever play scheme we provided. Her application was a little late, but she had written such a warm accompanying letter, we decided to interview her anyway. As it turned out, Sharon has been employed ever since that time and 15 years on is the Services Co-ordinator of SNAP. She came to SNAP having spent a considerable time nursing her elderly mother and has proved to be a highly valued worker. Sharon has also worked on an 'ad hoc' basis in our home caring for Andrew on a 1:1 level and she is well respected by all staff and children.

I felt that my time in SNAP was beginning to come to an end. SNAP had been the baby I had birthed, but now it was walking and talking. I knew that my development role was nearing completion. It took a huge amount of resolve, reflection and emotion to recognise it was time to disengage. How could I leave SNAP? I had given up my beloved Piano Teaching Practice for SNAP and now I was thinking of leaving? It had been so much part of my life and the life of my family and so many of my friends and parent's friends had become involved.......Yet I knew, deep within my inner consciousness that the time was coming for me to move on. Development work and Management work are two very different skills and I was now in the management phase. My season in SNAP was closing and this is often a very difficult time for any Development Officer to recognise that time and move out. As I felt this strong feeling within me, I recall taking home a few personal items out of my office drawer, just as the start of me disengaging from the role at the helm.

During this reflective time, various After School Clubs in the Out of School Federation were asking for training on special needs. As a result, the Federation secured funding to do a one year pilot project to develop a course which matched a National Certificate Module in special needs and would provide accredited training.

As the 'Playwork Industry' developed, it has become increasingly important to provide accredited training and eventually all clubs will require to have some staff who have SVQ Playwork or an associated qualification. The SNAP development phase had also incorporated a fair amount of personal study for me. Burning the midnight oil was a common occurrence during those years. I studied Higher National Certificate in Social Care, Scottish Vocational Qualification(SVQ)2 Playwork and SVQ4 Management. I wanted SNAP to be professional and believe that training is one aspect, which promotes professionalism within the workplace and causes staff to evaluate their occupational competence and practice.

So a few months later, the time came for me to move on. We had a farewell 'do' and one parent wrote and read a lovely poem. I looked around and saw a sea of faces – children with all kinds of special needs enjoying themselves, parents who had made friends with each other, staff who had come to love the jobs they did and lots of volunteers who gave their time freely to the cause. We had lots of wonderful play equipment, our staff proudly wore their T shirts with the SNAP logo which Julie had designed, we now had a Service Level Agreement with the Council and also owned our own mini bus. I felt a great sense of satisfaction and fulfilment that I had given five years of my life to such an important and valuable cause. Now it was time to hand it over to others who would take it forward and continue the good work which had been done.

I left SNAP and took on two part time jobs. One job was delivering training all over Highland on Special Needs and the other was working in the Merkinch Community Centre, which was classed as a Regeneration area. Both jobs proved to be very meaningful and valuable, as I took all the development skills with me into both jobs.

My networking had resulted in sitting on various strategic committees, at pan-Highland level and I also have been a member of the National Children's committee for Enable. Work included some development with colleagues to form a new Highland Children's Forum which acts as a conduit for parents and organisational views to be reflected to Statutory Agencies and comment on a wide range of consultative exercises and documents. I also continued to study and completed SVQ3 in Vocational Training and subsequently a Diploma in Health and Social Welfare with the Open University and since then I studied Counselling and a Personal performance Diploma in Life Coaching.

Marilyn Armstrong took on the position of SNAP Manager for a time and developed the Project further, with SNAPPIE suppers - cooking and having tea together and occasional sleepovers in the hall, all of which have been hugely successful. Once again, engineering these social occasions in the children's lives, which would happen normally in a mainstream world was paramount in their limited social worlds. Marilyn subsequently went to work abroad and Mairi Beaton, the supportive parent Board Member capably took over at the helm and she has taken the Organisation on further, developing the Young Adult club, through updating the Constitution and has given many years of her life to SNAP as has several other parents. I am so proud that SNAP is still flourishing today with many new Staff, Volunteers and Board Members.

SNAP is a vivid example of *tragedy to triumph*.

'Where there is a will, there is a way' and there was certainly a way to see the 'silent doorbells' ring again, just in a different way! It's not to say that all the pain disappeared, it just made the journey easier, more bearable and brought fun into life, in spite of the sadness.

Parties are usually fun events, but an emotional party happened on Wednesday 2nd July 2003 when a farewell SNAP party was provided for Andrew and his friend Gavin. Lots of party games were played and a farewell cake inscribed with both of their names. On Gavin's side of the cake with a tractor and Andrew's side with bagpipes, their particular interests in life. The hankies were wet, with tears of parting and of joy, since Andrew was really the start of SNAP.

The boys have grown up, they have become adults.

I had the pleasure of delivering the summer play scheme training to a group of eighteen SNAP staff two days later...... I counted it a high privilege to witness the ongoing good work of a wonderful organisation which is still flourishing today.

Dark clouds are sunbeam makers

11. Growing up

Child development is a fascinating process to follow. All the ages and stages - learning, exploring, asking and growing. Andrew physically developed at a normal pace and was growing into a fine looking young man with dark eyes, dark hair and slightly sallow skin. Lots of people commented about his charming smiles, which are flashed to everyone, even although no words are spoken, it is such an engaging way to communicate.

I referred earlier to *coping with loss* and had gone through the grieving process. However I recognised a process of 'progressive grief'. This term is sometimes used in the journey to acceptance – being progressive until the person reaches acceptance. Coming to a place of *acceptance* was very important for me. To come to a place where I was not always looking around every corner for a cure and having a clear perception of Andrew's ability. It was important for my emotional wholeness and as a result, my capacity to secure what was best for his life and future. I still grappled with big questions about how some people don't get any hardship and others get more than their fair share. Some people get cured and others don't. I still don't have answers to these big questions and still have conversations with trusted friends about core beliefs. I have often mused and reflected on all the prayers – what purpose did it all serve? Perhaps Andrew may have been much worse without these prayers, who knows......But I had to come to terms with the fact that no big healing miracle came his way and accept that this was our lot in life and learn to deeply love and accept Andrew for who he was, not who I wanted him to be.

This is also true of all our children as they grow up. Many people I have counselled or coached have talked to me about parents pushing them into careers which were not their choice. Also how parents can continue to be controlling in their adulthood and put on pressure with unrealistic expectations. I tell them *'Be yourself. Do what you want to do with your life'*. As a parent, it is so important to get the right balance, with gentle encouragement, listening ear, always ready to dialogue with our offspring, but also reminding them that *it is their choice and decisions, what they do with their life.* We all should have that opportunity to grow up, be independent and empowered to make our own decisions in life.

There were some occasions during these years, which I wish to share as they were significant and poignant in my journey of *'progressive grief'.* I remember one day walking along the High Street of Inverness and seeing a few local lads in town without an adult. They would be about 11 years old and just reaching that independent stage, of travelling to town on the bus and hanging around the computer or music stores. Suddenly my eyes glistened with tears as I realised that Andrew had not reached this level of independence and also posed the question in my mind – "would he ever reach that stage?" It was a sad day as I began to grapple with these issues of unreached milestones.

When Andrew reached adolescence, I realised he was growing up, had become a teenager, coupled with all the joys and sorrows, tears and tantrums, yet his mind still had this pre-school, concrete thinking where there was very little logic attached to the conversation. Occasional outbursts of violence really frightened me and at times, I wondered if I could continue to cope with this unpredictable behaviour. I needed help, but from where?

114

Thankfully, a few more sessions with the Clinical Psychologist helped me frame his behaviours and manage my emotional responses.

As Andrew was growing through his teenage years, we felt that it was important that he had other people caring for him in his life alongside his parents. We are very thankful to Dennis and Hilary Hopkins who provided a few years of regular one night per week respite for Andrew which gave us a night's sleep and some time off from the endless demands of caring, as he regularly woke up through the night and often with seizures. Staff who do this kind of work are golden treasures.

During these teenage years, coping with the unexpected was always a difficult challenge for me. Although Andrew had this uncontrolled epilepsy, it often took me by surprise and gave me such a shock. On one occasion, George and Andrew came to the railway station to meet me after being away on a work trip. As I stepped off the train, being near the front of the train, Andrew saw me and came running towards me to offer his usual enthusiastic hug. However as he ran forward, he took a major drop attack and fell forward right at the edge of the platform beside the train. My heart lurched from joy to sadness as we had to deal with the seizure, the position where he was lying, the injury from the seizure and explain to the train guard who thought that it was a fight and someone had punched him to the ground!

Other occasions while sitting in church listening to the minister, suddenly Andrew has a seizure which has caused some unexpected distraction to quietness of the atmosphere! Swimming was always something which we encouraged Andrew to do throughout his childhood years but as he got older, if he had a seizure in the swimming pool, it was very difficult to manage.

Also in cafes and restaurants, I always desperately hoped that he would not have a seizure, as it is such a confined place sitting at tables eating and then causing immense distress all round if he has a seizure, where people are looking on and the ensuing mayhem of spilled drinks or food. Dealing with these unexpected situations in public places constantly caught me by surprise and still does to this day evoking sadness watching the effects of the condition. However, I would always weigh up the possibility versus the experience of Andrew having a quality of life and if I had to add up the amount of times he had seizures in public places it would be about 10% of the time as most would occur at home on waking and after his day's activity.

In the church we attended at that time, there was a large group of young people. Generally, Andrew was alone. Occasionally a young person may venture a few words with him. One Sunday, there was a 16th birthday lunch after church. As usual, Andrew wasn't invited and we drove off home after the service. During the afternoon, Andrew was cutting up bits of paper in his bedroom. When I enquired what game he was playing, he replied by saying *"I'm making tickets for the party"*. My heart was so sad yet again at the exclusion. He had understood the information that a party was on, but he was excluded and he was trying to include himself. Oh the pain and anguish of being on the outside! Not being invited or included and knowing you are not included, but at home in your own room, trying in some tiny way to include yourself. Oh the sadness and hurt re-inforced yet again!

One appointment with the Community Paediatrician brought another short bout of grief as I explored my response to that meeting. She was a warm lady, listened and was very professional. I had suggested that when Andrew leaves school at 19 yrs he was around 15yrs on this occasion, perhaps he could get a job as a trolley boy in a large supermarket. The Paediatrician looked deeply into my eyes with empathy and intuitively commented that employers would not take on the responsibility of having someone with uncontrolled epilepsy and severe learning difficulties.

I was again reeling. My eyes stung with tears. How could I be so naïve to expect that this was possible? Did I still not understand the severity of his condition at fifteen years old? I suppose that I hadn't quite realised that Andrew had higher support needs. After all, he was my son, we got on with life, but this was a different agenda. The future was looming and what could his life become? I did not want him to go to a Day Centre, which was under-resourced and over populated. He would have something different, appropriate, stimulating, meeting his needs, out in community somewhere, but I didn't know how that could come about.

So it was another short period of grief for me as I started to realise that Andrew's future had a higher support element than I had imagined. Oh dear, this was somehow another blow to my wounded heart yet again. I thought I had it all framed neatly and understood the situation and prognosis, yet I had to walk that path again of grief into acceptance, that his future would be dependent on others. At least these periods of grief were shorter, not years but months instead, processing the concepts, adapting expectations yet again and coming to a new place of acceptance.

Coping with change and adapting to a new set of social rules can be uncomfortable and I recall meeting with the Psychiatrist to discuss Andrew's teenage behaviours which we felt we were not coping or managing to deal with and respond in the best way. We needed help and advice from the specialist.

Our ethos regarding discipline in the home was based on respect for one another and authentic communication to resolve issues of conflict. However, since Andrew was a 'child in his mind', we could not have these logical discussions and often we would get into unrealistic altercations in trying to reason with him, especially when he began to insist that he wasn't going out with us on a trip, or shopping or for a walk. This created a huge annoyance for us and we were not coping well as this teenager was making it clear to us what he 'did not want to do' and often it would be to his benefit rather than staying home playing endlessly with lego or watching videos.

The Psychiatrist came to see us and told us 'back off' and walk away from any potential altercation with Andrew. In withdrawing from any potential conflicting situation, this would minimise angst and allow calm to return. It also meant that *we would have to adjust our expectations* in what we did with our time and how we spent it together. He also told us quite candidly that we should go on our holidays abroad on our own. He questioned the value of taking Andrew abroad and was it really meaningful for him?

Well that was a real biggie for us! For the past number of years we had always taken him abroad with us but latterly when he was 16 years old, we were at a beautiful hotel in

Menorca, all he wanted to do was sit in the bedroom playing with his cards or play on the toy horse for young children in the bar area. We felt that neither was appropriate and after planning an expensive holiday, it turned out to be quite a disaster all round.

The following year we took him to Madeira, a beautiful island on the Canaries and while out walking one day he had a drop attack which is an atonic seizure where he suddenly drops down to the ground with tremendous force and both his front teeth were chipped and damaged. This caused me huge stress as I was concerned each time we went abroad about having to visit the doctor or hospital and communicating in a foreign language.

Andrew had numerous admissions to casualty as a result of falling down with seizures and getting lots of head injuries, which was highly stressful to deal with and also trying to communicate with health staff who didn't understand the severity of his learning disability since *'he looked fine'* and so his condition on the surface was frequently misunderstood. On a few occasions my sister came with us on holiday and she helped to care for him, which was greatly appreciated and this shared care enabled us to get some time to ourselves.

So, when listening to the Learning Disability Psychiatrist's advice it made sense to me. George was very reluctant about the idea, but we were encouraged to continue to send him to Badaguish Respite Centre in Aviemore which he loved, and that would probably be more meaningful all round for him and for us. It was a big step when we eventually decided to go abroad just as a couple, *but we did enjoy ourselves* and the new feeling of going away without him was broken in. In some ways it was another step in that 'progressive grief' that sense of letting go of expectations, enjoying holidays together and realigning our dreams and aspirations. We have subsequently enjoyed several holidays abroad just as a couple and indeed it provided the refreshment that we needed during those years to continue in our caring roles.

Since I had a wide network of contacts in the Voluntary and Statutory Sector, I spoke with the Senior Social Worker for Families with disability. I requested that a Transition Working Group should be initiated, to explore future services for young people. The Scottish Executive Report had published a review called *'The Same as You'* which suggested that young people leaving school should no longer be placed in Day Centres. Obviously, I wanted to know what alternatives could be provided and also desired to be involved in influencing that debate and process. The Senior Social Worker and her senior colleague set up a Transition Working Group which gained considerable momentum and attracted a range of professionals around the table to debate these challenging issues.

Time was ticking away and all too soon, 12th August 2002 would be there on the calendar, it would be Andrew's 18th Birthday. We always celebrated his birthday as a family, but he wanted a *party* on this special occasion. Who could I invite? He was never invited to parties. The only party I ever remember was when he was eight years old the little girl up the street invited all the children into her house for a party the mum was happy to have Andrew. I was on hand if she needed my help. But now, it would be his 18th and he wanted a party, who would we invite?

Who would run it, as I would probably be an emotional wreck seeing my lovely big son, now a man and yet a child in his mind. I talked with the FALCON Project, which

120

is a weekly leisure club for young adults with learning disabilities and asked if they would come to the party. Would they come? We couldn't hold them back!

Every week Andrew attended the club, we had to go through how long it would be until the party, where it was being held, who was attending, what we would be doing and eating of course! The FALCON Project Leader provided the disco, which was brilliant.

The Active Adults Group from the Merkinch Community Centre prepared and served the buffet. Friends and family decorated the building and set up the PA equipment. It was truly a fantastic evening. About 60 people came to the party. Family, friends, school friends, SNAP friends, parents and of course all the FALCON members. We danced the whole night. Even a piper from the Community Centre piped in the Birthday cake, which really made the night for Andrew as he loves Scottish pipe bands.

I had no tears as I was a happy and proud mum.

We celebrated in style and Andrew was looking a fine handsome young man with his friends around him, yes, his friends were people who all had learning disabilities but we were not alone, we were all together, enjoying one another and having fun. Everyone who came along gave such beautiful and thoughtful gifts. The party video has been played hundreds of times by Andrew, remembering his special day.

There was an additional special moment for our family.....Julie's South African boyfriend Michael Mortimer came to the party. He was tall and handsome, quietly confident, very accepting and at ease with Andrew. It was our first occasion to meet him – he was such a natural with all the different people with disabilities, even although he had no experience in this field. He danced the night away too, but had a special glint in his eye for our daughter, Julie.

He was fast becoming a member of our family too!

Success is the ability to go from one failure to another with no loss of enthusiasm
Winston Churchill

12. Becoming an Adult

Andrew was now a man. His friends at FALCON club told him every week for months, that he was now a man and *he could go to the pub*, now that he had his 18th birthday. I am not too sure if that was his primary understanding of growing up! It was becoming increasingly apparent that he was outgrowing school and the SNAP Project. The SNAP Family Christmas party was held as usual in the Smithton Free Church hall. It was a very happy occasion with children there from 5 years old, right up through to the older teenagers. Mum and Dads, Siblings, Friends, SNAP Staff and Volunteers. There were lots of fun party games but Andrew would not join in any of them. He was the tallest lad there and seemed quite withdrawn. Various people spoke to him, but he was choosing not to answer their friendly greetings.

My heart had yet another sad shadow. I knew what this meant......Andrew was outgrowing SNAP. I talked with many of the parents, who chatted about the stages of their children, sharing little pockets of progress with me. I tried to rejoice with them but my heart felt heavy.

I so longed to be able to share some progress about Andrew, but all I could share was the fact that he was growing into a man. Other than that, there was no real progress, yet their learning disabled children were slowly showing some progress. The party continued. A lovely buffet was provided by a parent and her friend, what a feast. Andrew was not withdrawn when it came to eating! He had a good appetite and made full use of it. Later in the evening, Santa arrived and a present was lovingly given to every child. Such joy, laughter and fun! Andrew did go and receive his gift with a smile, but was ready to leave as soon as possible.

As I left the happy atmosphere of inclusion, belonging and acceptance, I desperately fought back a rushing river of tears as I realised he had outgrown the SNAP Project. He was walking through the avenue of transition into adulthood and I had to find a new place of inclusion, belonging and acceptance. Life goes on, it does not stand still. I came home that evening and had a long reflective and tearful session. I was thinking, musing, considering and reflecting on all the chapters of Andrew's life until now. In a strange way, I didn't want it to end. Once again, I had to deal with my emotions, embrace change and be the best mum I could be for my son as he journeyed his way into adulthood.

The party experience re-inforced transition, passage into adulthood, the requirement for new social opportunities and the need to face the future. Although Andrew was still in school, two of his days were now spent at the local College attending a special needs course on vocational subjects. He had an auxiliary helper from the school supporting him on one day and on the second day a member of staff had been released from the local day centre to support him. That was not without its problems – lots of lobbying, challenging, assertive phone calls, e mails and meetings in order to receive the second day of support for Andrew at college. If I had not taken this action, he would not have been able to access the place. The issue being that he was still in school and not in full time social work care. However, he had been transferred to Social Work Adult Services from the Children's Team but somehow the two didn't connect!

The Transition Working Group became much more dominant in my agenda. There had been lots of valuable discussion around the polished table and I was no longer intimidated but was nicely assertive and could articulate my thoughts with ease. Each interest group had prepared a paper on Service Provision gaps and how they could be met. We had convened a conference in the Highland Council Chamber on Transition, which was well attended. The Development Manager from Enable in Glasgow gave the guest presentation on a new *without walls* service in the central belt of Scotland. We had already visited some services in Glasgow and Lanarkshire where Enable were developing creative services which were very personalised. I gave a power point presentation on Andrew's transition journey with lots of photographs, giving an emotive challenge about support and new services required for the future.

It was my impression that the Highland Council in principle, supported new development of day care services. However, it did seem that time was ticking away and there were few, if any appropriate options for those who had complex needs.

During this time a new initiative was being launched on a national basis called *Direct Payments.* This was a system whereby the Local Authority would give funds rather than direct service provision and the user could purchase a service themselves. This was based on the social model of disability, which is about empowerment and choice for the disabled person. They can choose who they want to employ, how they will provide the service, when they want to receive that service and as a result, effectively becoming employers.

It seemed to me that, this could be a potential route for us as a family to explore. We could still retain our weekly overnight respite care from our long term committed carers Dennis and Hilary Hopkins. Andrew loved to go there for his meal and stay overnight, then he would go on to school the next day. Our thanks to them will remain forever, in that they were willing to provide this highly valuable service to us as a family and just gave us that little break every week. We could still purchase care from Crossroads if we wanted to and also employ people who knew Andrew well and were trained in the field.

Our Care Manager was supportive and professional. She was thorough in her assessment procedures and went off to collate all the information about Direct Payments. Later she returned armed with various booklets and information. One booklet was very detailed, while another was simply produced with pictures and very little text. This meant that it was user-friendly for Andrew, since he could not read. The Community Care assessment was done for the Direct Payment and subsequently approved. It was not long before the first cheque came through our letterbox. A new bank account had to be opened, we recruited our own staff and a payroll system set up with a local company. We were ready to roll right into a new way of delivering a community care service for our son.

Direct Payments brought some normality to our lives. We could organise staff to come when we required them, not fitting into a regular time frame which was previously offered. If we planned to go off for a week-end, we organised staff and Andrew's life could carry on as normal. I became a 'champion' of Direct Payments, felt empowered and Andrew too was very happy with the arrangements. As a result of this very positive experience, I worked part time for a voluntary organisation called

'Direct Payments Scotland' and travelled around seven Local Authority areas supporting Local Authorities, Voluntary Organisations and Individuals to implement this new system of providing social care.

This was Andrew's last year in school. Most Secondary Schools have school trips away, sometimes abroad or at least in UK which can include learning and socialising, developing independence. Alas this was not so for Andrew and his peers. Some of them did go off for an overnight and some also had the opportunity of attending work placements, but this was not on offer for Andrew. I felt that he at least should be given some kind of opportunity to have a work placement so that the idea of leaving school could be re-inforced to him as this would be a major transition for him. Nothing was offered.

So I decided to ask Bob and Helen Bull, who ran a small croft and were developing a project for special needs, if Andrew could come for a week work placement. They agreed that it would be possible but he would require to bring his own support with him. I asked the school if they could release an auxiliary from the classroom to go with him, but this was not possible. Oh dear, what else could I try? I rang the local Day Centre and asked if one of their staff could support him, but no, apparently he was not on their books as he was still at school, almost 19yrs, however the irony of this matter was that adult social work services started at 18yrs.

My frustration at the system was building – how could I get the appropriate support for this to happen? I was not giving up on this as I felt it was really important! I asked my social worker if we could use some of our Direct Payments Funds to pay one of our own staff to support him and it was agreed. So thankfully, Andrew did get his work placement on the croft. It was lambing season and he loved feeding the lambs with bottles, moving bales of hay and doing other various tasks around the farm. After the placement was finished, I asked him "What did you enjoy about the farm" and very clearly he replied with these words which I will never forget "Working hard". I knew that day, that he was emotionally ready to leave school.

The months were ticking by quickly and there was still no option of a new creative service for Andrew and those like him. Lots more meetings and discussions about what could be possible, but nothing concrete. By this time, there were two other parents who had sons in the same category and all three of us were becoming increasingly concerned about the future of our sons after leaving special school in the summer. It was mid-May when we decided that the best route to have this creative stimulating service, would be to have a full Direct Payment Package and also apply for Independent Living Fund (ILF). This meant that outside funds from ILF Central Government Funds could be levered in order to increase the level of service provision for our sons.

Time was not on our side. These applications take some time to be processed. ILF will not be approved until the Local Authority had given a commitment of their funds to the client. It felt like we were once again swirling around in a state of confusion, being fed different messages from various Council Officers. I had to put on my lobbying hat yet again! The local Councillor was contacted, as was the Director of Social Work, in order to secure a decision on the Direct Payment for a full and holistic service. Our anxiety levels were rapidly escalating as time was running out fast. It was only two weeks until Andrew was leaving school, we received an e mail to confirm that the Direct Payment had been officially approved!

Andrew enjoyed his many end of term celebrations, garden party, disco and college presentation. At last the day arrived when he finished school. For several days that followed, Andrew kept saying to me *"I've left school"*. The penny had dropped in his mind. He understood what was happening that he was moving on from school into an adult world. He was now a man and no longer a teenager, he had left school and he was ready to face the next season of his life.

This came as a surprise to me, as I didn't think he would really grasp the concept of leaving school and I was concerned about how this transition would go for him, but he was really pleased with himself that he had left school. I think he was ready after all.

The foolish man seeks happiness in the distance,
the wise grows it under his feet.
James Openheim

13. Post School Years

Yes Andrew had officially left school and what would his life look like now? We had managed to secure a good Direct Payments / Independent Living Fund Package but now we had the responsibility of managing the money, recruiting staff and arranging an appropriate programme for Andrew to attend meaningful activities each day. It was a fair amount of responsibility and like running a small scale business. Some staff were already on board on a part time basis during the last while at school so they were happy to take on more hours. However, it was important that we had a team, so that there would be a 'bank' of people to draw on if someone was off sick or on holiday.

Although George had taken early retirement at 50yrs from his BT job as an engineer, he still wanted to 'have a life' and became involved in Children's Panel voluntary work and also Citizen's Advice Bureau as a volunteer. He had taken on the role of 'main carer' and I was working full time. He has been an excellent carer to Andrew and excelled as a man at caring, washing, cleaning, organising and also doing all the associated administration. I helped out to a lesser extent as I had become very tired being the full time carer until Andrew reached 16yrs. So the system worked well for us at home and we clearly understood each other's roles.

It was very important to us that Andrew went out every day to do some meaningful and preferably physical work which he enjoyed each day. Tailoring a programme to HIS needs was paramount, not what we wanted but what would suit him. So it took some time to get a full five day timetable organised for his activities. Eventually the programme looked like this:

Monday – Glachbeg Croft doing farm tasks, cleaning out the hen houses, collecting eggs. In the afternoon they would bake as a group and enjoy eating some too!
Evening: Out to SNAP young adults club with friends – they had now developed a new club for this age group which was wonderful, as he could enjoy these friendships.

Tuesday – Co-op packing the crisps and biscuits. Horse riding in the afternoon.
Evening: FALCON Club where he met lots of other adults with learning disabilities.

Wednesday – Floral Hall, a supported gardening project. In the afternoon, he would go back to the croft with Bob and have a literacy session, with writing and hearing a story being read to him.
Bob's club in the evening

Thursday – L'Arche sawing wood into small kindlers. He enjoyed all the socialising with all the others who attend the project.

Friday - Feeding the ducks and visit to the library, work on the PC then in the afternoon he would go again to Bob at the Croft and have his literacy session.

Saturday - out with family for lunch

Sunday – Church called Inverness Christian Fellowship, where he is accepted well and then home to Mum and Dad's for Sunday lunch.

Bob Bull and his wife Helen, who is a senior teacher at Drummond Special School are so dedicated to the cause of learning disability. They bought a croft and developed a whole project around providing a day time service to all kinds of children and adults with additional needs. Andrew was their first daytime 'client' and it has been a real haven for him, like a second home! On some occasions Bob and Helen would take Andrew for a week-end to let George and me go off for a short break together. We shall always be most grateful to them for all their support to our family.

Supporting Andrew's activity programme took *a lot of time and effort.* It was indeed like running a small business with a team of staff to organise, keep records of all the hours for their wages and also ensure that all the bills were paid to the various projects. Bob Bull from Glachbeg helped us with the co-ordination of the programme as some services closed over the summer and alternative activities had to be found. This was a great support to us.

Occasionally we would have team meetings with all the staff to discuss how things were going and staff would learn little strategies from one another – especially around the issues of managing any occasional un-cooperative behaviours. Usually Andrew would respond to humour, or having plenty warning beforehand, or cues such as: shoes sitting beside his couch as a reminder *'you are going out soon'* or just being left to do the task in his own time, rather than our time! So the planning and facilitating of these Team Meetings all took up time to discuss all of these issues.

At the week-ends George would often take Andrew out for a snack at lunch time on Saturday while I got on with the 'homey stuff' since I worked full time. It took him out for a few hours, otherwise he would stay all day in his sitting room playing with his cars and lego only coming out for his dinner, so stimulation was a very important key. On one occasion we sent him to a Respite Unit where he never came out his room for a whole week, but only to eat. He was withdrawn, sad, un-shaven and said he didn't want to go back. Needless to say, we never sent him there again.....

However, he did love to go to Badaguish, just outside Aviemore which is a ten bedded Respite Unit for people with learning disabilities out in the country. They provide lots of outdoor activities and Andrew did love their dog, so they allowed him to have the dog sleeping on the floor of his room. It is a lovely facility with a large wooden style lodge, having the Cairngorm Mountains as a backdrop. He attended the unit since he was ten years old and has enjoyed many short breaks there. They do a wonderful job!

He also enjoyed attending the Scripture Union Camp in Pitlochry which was run for teenagers with special needs. That was a wonderful week where he was buddied on a 1:1 basis and they had a full programme of interesting activities.

When the camps were no longer available for Andrew, I started asking around to find what else was on offer and discovered a wonderful organisation called Prospects. It is a Christian national charity which provides services for people with learning disabilities and enables them to have a specialist church service. We went to our first ever Prospects meeting in Edinburgh and I knew from the start of the first song that Andrew belonged there! There was such a natural sense of inclusion, acceptance and simplicity. Subsequently,

I became involved in setting up an Inverness Prospects group which meets once per month and we go to the Scottish National Week-end each year and meet up with all the old friends from Prospects and from Scripture Union Camp.

Latterly, as previously mentioned, Auntie Elizabeth also took Andrew for week-end breaks and she always provided interesting outings and activities to do with him. He loved his visits there and all the fun she had with the furry monkey!

Choices are the hinges of destiny

14. Independence

During the teenage years of development, occasionally the conversation would emerge about "future adult life for our sons and daughters". However, these conversations would be short and fleeting as few people wanted to face the biggest transition of all. Transitions happen throughout our lives, one of the biggest when we enter the world from the safety of our mother's womb into the big world with all its new sights, smells, noises and experiences. To follow on, comes the expected developmental phases of walking, talking and learning to take care of ourselves. Alas, for many of us parents, we do not see and experience these developmental milestones and constantly have to adjust our expectations for our child along life's journey.

Many children, go to nursery, primary school, secondary school, get a Saturday job and then begin to pursue the career of their choice through employment or further study. This season usually develops independence of living in shared accommodation with other young adults until life secures the opportunities of having complete independence from parental care and developing social relationships or connections to live the lifestyle of their choice. What of our sons and daughters with learning disabilities? What choice do they have? What provisions and strategy is in place for their futures?

As previously mentioned the transition from special school is a big transition finding suitable activities and support for daily life, but the *big question* still lurks in the backgrounds of all our minds, *'where will he live in the future'?*

Having attended numerous Committee Meetings and Conferences on learning disability, I had heard some sad stories of parents keeping their son or daughter until the parent died and suddenly the person is hurriedly removed from the familiar family home to a residential or shared house situation, with no planning or preparation. Needless to say, this action can produce depression, deeper grief, loss and also present some very challenging behaviour for the person with the learning disability, as they don't understand what has happened in their lives.

We always felt that Andrew would move out from the family home when we began to reach 60yrs old. Conversations were opened with Social Work about Andrew's future and we were encouraged to look at some of the residential homes in Inverness. We visited several, but felt that a sizeable residential home did not provide the 1:1 care which Andrew required around his unpredictable seizure disorder. The conclusion we came to, was that Andrew would be best placed in his own home.

I attended a 'Transitions Event' in Drummond School which was a very well organised event run by Helen Bull, the Senior Teacher who worked in that field within the school. She had around 30 different organisations represented at the event. There was a stall from Albyn Housing and I decided to have a chat with the lady. I told her that Andrew had been on the housing waiting list since he had left Drummond School (6 years) and I wondered when he may be allocated a house? She told me that *'he would just be on the list with the other 10,000 people who were on the list'.* I really couldn't believe what I was hearing! Did they not have some specialist list for all our young adults coming up to that stage?

It didn't seem like it! I was in shock that there were no options for housing, no information for adults with special needs and it seemed to me as if there was no planning for all their future accommodation. Fifty years before, all of those people were relegated to a large institution and they were cared for all their days. Nowadays they live at home with no planning for adult accommodation? I found this unbelievable and truly difficult to comprehend. I had fully expected that Andrew's name would be on a specialist list somewhere and that a strategy would be in place for all the young adults who were coming up and possible places or building programmes planned for the future. Apparently not. I was not tearful by now, but very disappointed that I had entered into yet another maze – the housing and accommodation maize where there appeared to be inadequate planning and preparation.

My husband and I both met with the Albyn Housing lady again to discuss the matter further but apparently, there was no list and no plans...........She encouraged me to write to Head of Policy in the Council, which I did, but that shed no real light on the matter. We were also informed that Andrew would require a 'housing assessment' even although he had been assessed all his life, but this was about the physical environment. I then had to search around to find out who did this specific assessment and I wrote to the Community Occupational (OT) Service to ask if this could be done. Within a short time, a lovely and very efficient OT came from the Community OT Service for Learning Disability and did a very thorough assessment of what Andrew would require if he was living in his own home. So at least that was something else in place, in readiness for when 'the house' would become available. In fact, she and her colleagues proved to be a great support during the final phase.

I hoped, imagined, believed and visualised Andrew in his own little house, preferably in the village of North Kessock where we live. I used to imagine what life could be like, not having to rush home all the time 'to be back for the carer'. I imagined what life could be like, where I could work late if I needed or wanted to, or go shopping, or go for a swim, without being bound by carer's hours. We could even plan week-ends away and holidays without the worry and concern of how care for Andrew could be worked out. After all, I had now been caring for 32 years since Julie had been born.

One day when I was driving out of our village, North Kessock I saw a builder's sign at the roundabout before driving on to the dual carriageway. I decided to stop on my way home and check it out. The sign was Tulloch, a large locally based building company who were starting the first phase of their building project in the village. I had heard that with any housing building project, there is a requirement for some element of Social Housing - I used to call it 'Council Housing'.

I wrote a letter to the Development Manager of Tulloch telling him about Andrew and asked if he could point me in the right direction please. He replied promptly, telling me that Cairn Housing was the Social Housing provider and to contact their Development Manager. After several attempts at phoning - he has a *very* busy job, he spoke with me and set up a meeting. I told him all about Andrew's needs and he said that his Organisation had never worked with people who had learning difficulties but was open to it, so would speak to his Chief Executive.

A further meeting was arranged with the Development Manager and the Chief Executive to discuss Andrew's case. George and I went to the Cairn Housing Offices

141

and we were taken into the Board Room. On the large board room table lay the plans for the North Kessock Development and they said to us *"What house would you like for Andrew".* I am sure you can imagine my sheer delight at being able to choose what house we wanted for our son! There were various blocks of flats on the development and four lovely little two bed roomed bungalows – we chose a bungalow for Andrew.

The next step was for Social Work to open discussions with Cairn Housing as there would be negotiations regarding tenancy, rent and of course 24/7 care package. After that meeting, there was a very, very long wait. Our own Social Worker, although very supportive and informed wasn't kept in the loop and she could rarely tell us what was happening with the houses. Negotiations took months longer than we anticipated. The Highland Council decided to take all four bungalows which meant that four people would be allocated a house and the Council would provide the care packages. After that decision was taken, it was reversed and put out to tender. The Richmond Fellowship won the tender, they then had to recruit and train staff, which took even more time.

We also had to go through the process of securing Welfare Guardianship for Andrew and we, as his 'legal guardians' would be signing the tenancy agreement for his house. The guardianship process was lengthy and very bureaucratic, although I understand the reasons why, but we had to tell the Mental Health Officer why we were appropriate guardians. Forms stating Andrew's incapacity from our GP and a Specialist Consultant had to be secured, as had recommendations from our regular care worker and our daughter. The Solicitor was very compassionate and understanding, which really helped and supported us during that very invasive process. On the 8th February 2011 we were granted Legal Guardianship of our son Andrew Normington.

We had hoped that Andrew would have moved into his home by Christmas 2010 but not so.....the Highland Council wheels turn slowly and there seemed to be endless meetings and emails about the move. Eventually, the date was agreed 9th April 2011 – he would be first to move into the beautiful new bungalows. We spent a fair amount of money getting it all kitted out to a high spec. – we wanted the best for him. We purchased a lovely couch which reclined and could be useful when Andrew had a seizure and needed a nap. A lovely double bed with cream, red and brown duvet and matching curtains was bought for his bedroom. All the quality white goods were bought for the kitchen including a solid oak table and chairs.

Family and friends bought various items for the kitchen and Andrew had some furniture from his own little sitting room which fitted nicely into his lounge. There was a short transition period of around three weeks where the carers would take him up to the house for little visits and he would gradually leave some lego, cars, jigsaws, cuddly teddies – all his special stuff. Then the big day arrived.

I had regularly told myself, I would not grieve over this move. I had done all my grieving and we had carefully planned this transition and I was ready for it and I believed Andrew was too.

The day dawned very misty and George went to town and collected the hired transit van. Andrew had a seizure around 7.45am so he slept again and then got up about 8.30am. He was in great spirits and looking forward to his move. He helped move all his boxes of possessions into the van, with his blue and ash furniture from his little sitting room. The sun shone through into a lovely day and as soon as we reached the house he wanted the CD player going with Glen Miller jazzy music booming out the brassy joyful sound. We were all grinning at his evident joy and gladness!

Very quickly, the house had Andrew's stamp on it – all his things that were precious to him round about him. We had the old Nintendo hooked up to his favourite car game and he was very happy sitting on his new couch playing his computer game. Michael our son-in-law is very handy and he was doing some DIY tasks in the house. George cut the grass front and back, then the place was complete. The Team Leader from Richmond Fellowship arrived to take over and we said goodbye, we'll see you tomorrow. Big hug *"Bye Mum, Bye Dad, Bye Michael, Bye Julie and Naomi"* and it was done.

Julie and I went off to town to have some lunch and some 'girlie retail therapy'. I didn't cry over Andrew and haven't since, as he is a man in his own home, living his own life to his full potential. He brings joy to us and we to him. However, I have had tears over Julie and Michael's wee girl Naomi, because she is severely disabled, with complex needs, severe visual impairment and requires high support, rarely sleeps and cries lots and has various other difficulties. My husband too has been diagnosed with terminal cancer, but these are other stories for another day.

Life certainly does not turn out the way we would want or expect, but as I look back there have been many valuable lessons and experiences along the way.

Sadly some of the wonderful activities which Andrew attended have been cut due to all the Local Authority cut backs. Richmond Fellowship are doing their utmost to keep Andrew active and occupied doing meaningful activities each day. Andrew settled in really well to his own home and hasn't looked back. In fact some people have commented that they think he has '*grown up a little bit*' well I hope it's true. I want the best for him and indeed for him to be all he can be while on this earth.

I am so thankful and grateful for the use of this lovely little two bed roomed bungalow given to Andrew for his own independent life.

Yesterday is gone.
Tomorrow has not yet come.
We have only today.
Let us begin.

Mother Teresa

15. Personal Reflection

As I look back over these twenty seven years of Andrew's life, it could have been quite different. If Andrew did not have a learning disability he could have studied for his chosen career in university, or learned a trade and be working at a good job, with his own money and his own flat and be in perfect health.

He could have lots of friends and a girl friend, or partner, or wife, owning and driving his own car or motorbike. He could have his own family and I could have had more grandchildren. He may have been a musician or singer or technician or mechanic. He may have chosen to travel around the world working in different countries or perhaps doing humanitarian work with a charity. The other side is that he could have been unemployed or addicted to alcohol, smoking or drugs and be homeless.

He isn't any of these and in fact he is Andrew – the unique person he was created to be for this time in the world. Yes he does still have a learning disability and complex uncontrolled epilepsy which is difficult to deal with, but that is his condition which has to be managed. He has to wear a hard hat wherever he goes because of the fact that he can drop down anywhere and we have to take his emergency bag with medication, emergency blanket and change of clothes everywhere we go, but that is who he is and we are all used to him wearing his hard hat.

His carers tell us that he is a joy to look after, this pleases us very much! He also has a 'girlfriend' Sharon who he sees from time to time. She lives in the village of Avoch and is the only girl he has ever 'taken a shine to' so that's really sweet. They send each other valentine cards and enjoy having an occasional trip out together with their carers. These are precious little life moments for both of them.

Every child is a gift to this world and Andrew was the gift to us and our family. Not only that, he is a gift to Inverness and Scotland. I have travelled all over Scotland delivering training and telling the story of Andrew and although he doesn't really know it or understand it, his story is quite far reaching – the gift he is to all of us. When I go to visit him at his house, he runs to the door and opens it with a big smile and nearly knocks me over with such an enthusiastic hug and says: *"hello mum"* and then very quickly becomes engrossed in his video again, so I am left talking to the carer, nevertheless I treasure these passing moments of love and joy with him.

Life does not always turn out the way we expect, but our *attitude* is paramount in how we respond to life. I could be a very embittered and angry mother feeling that life has let me down. I could have had an emotional breakdown and never recovered. I could have ended my life that day by the river. My marriage could have been completely broken forever. My life could be empty and lonely. I could be selfish and only think of myself and my family. I could be unemployed, de-motivated, lethargic, disillusioned and isolated.

I could still be teaching piano and doing what I always did in my little safe, cocooned world. I am not doing that, because I chose to go with the new doors which opened to me. I had a choice, just like we all have on a daily basis. I made a conscious decision to choose *not to be bitter but to be better* – allowing life's circumstances to change me and shape me into the woman I am meant to be.

It's not to say that I still don't have my struggles and questions, I still do, but now manage them much better and seek for the light and love rather than the grief and sadness. I really hate to see Andrew have seizures and when he has a dull day and not communicating, it can cause a shadow of sadness, but I try to look for the good each day and be thankful for the good things, adopting an 'attitude of gratitude'. I seek to support my daughter and her family as best as I can, trying to understand the pain and high demands of another disabled child in our family, to which there appears no answer. But she too is a GIFT to all of us in this world and time will tell as she grows, how her gift will teach us and give us valuable insights into life itself.

This is a part of my personal mission statement:

"To be a voice for those who have no voices"

This statement and decision has changed my career, introduced me to so many new friends and taught me so much about life and community development. I have made many friendships with parents in similar situations to our own family. I also enjoyed positive working relationships with a wide range of professionals who were involved in Andrew's life for which I am most thankful. The experience has taken me on a journey of learning I may never have chosen. Hardship and challenges have strengthened my marriage. I have learned about the importance of needing help from others and learning to be interdependent. My perception of carer's needs strengthened as I recognised the need and importance of accessing user-friendly professional psychology services.

The experience has introduced me to a wide variety of learning styles and experiences such as: committee work; public speaking, chairing meetings, networking with a wide range of organisations; doing Scottish Vocational Qualifications and being assessed by a workplace assessor; sitting in college as a mature student doing Higher National Certificate; studying an Open University Diploma on a distance learning basis; learning to write training materials and deliver training courses; writing presentations for conferences; lobbying politicians; talking with the press; organising conferences; writing business plans and funding applications; responding to many consultations and being involved in research and media; studying and delivering counselling and life coaching sessions.

Not only that, I had the privilege of setting up the SNAP Project and becoming a Development Officer. This led on to becoming a Freelance Trainer and also assisting to set up the Highland Children's Forum. I then travelled widely promoting Direct Payments to many people and organisations. All of these skills took me into the Merkinch Community Centre and delivering lots of new Project Developments, which include three projects in the Centre for Learning Disability and developed and installed a new Theatre Facility. I also run two singing groups: one for older people called *Singing for Pleasure* and one for adults with learning disabilities called *The Rainbow Singers,* both of which have waiting lists and are filled with dynamic positive energy as we share the joy of group singing together.

Since then, I set up the Inverness Prospects Group and trained as a Counsellor and Life Coach and recently set up a charity called 'Women Influencing Change' where we deliver confidence building to women who have a low self esteem and want to move forward in life with a programme called 'Reaching High' and to date numerous people have been helped and encouraged forward in their lives. Many of these women have moved from depression into volunteering or further training and indeed some have moved into employment. Since starting the 'Reaching High' programme I have developed another charity called Friends of the Therapy Suite (FOTS) with a local business, The Therapy Suite, to provide therapeutic sessions for disadvantaged women.

There are so many treasures in darkness.

You may recall, I talked about the light that began to appear in my dark cave. As I stepped towards the light, these treasure chests of life began to open up to me - yes many of them. Even as I type these words and read them on the screen, I realise afresh the treasure chests that have been opened to me through the gift of Andrew. A very important lesson I learned, was *to accept all people*, but particularly with learning disabilities on an equal basis to everyone else and value who they are and the contribution they make to society.

One of the most valuable treasures I found in my cave of darkness was the beauty and simplicity of the gift of human life. Regardless of talent, skill, ability and achievement, just the precious gift of life itself and how we interact as human beings, can transcend all barriers, disabilities, gender, ethnicity, religion and social backgrounds. It has been so valuable to learn to communicate without words, using smiles and gestures, body language and music to engage in meaningful dialogue as human beings. How precious this is to be in harmony - diverse people who care about each other.

The silent doorbell has changed my life, forever.

If I had not decided to be *'better and not bitter'* then I wonder how my life may have turned out.   Perhaps someone else may have come along and developed another kind of SNAP, who knows? However, I believe that it is imperative that we respond positively to our life circumstances and live *'in the flow of life'*. It may not be perfect or how we imagined, but a positive attitude and response can make all the difference. I sincerely trust that you have found some insight, encouragement and hope through reading my personal story, whether you are a parent, professional or interested reader.

The principle remains the same - *let's allow life's circumstances to make us better and discover these treasures in the darkness.*

Elsie Normington

Contact Details

To contact Elsie Normington for workshops or motivational speaking engagements:

E mail: elsien@uwclub.net

Mobile: 077 3495 8800

Web Links

www.thesilentdoorbell.com

www.enfoundation.co.uk

www.elsienormington.com

www.reachinghigh.net

www.snapinverness.com